The Yogi
the Commissar
and the Third-World Church

to
JANET
whose courage for new life
makes good news credible
and
new beginnings possible

The Yogi
the Commissar
and the Third-World Church

Paul Clasper

Judson Press, Valley Forge

Contents

1

The Pendulum-Swing
from Yogi to Commissar

Arthur Koestler has written a provocative essay called "The Yogi and the Commissar." [1] His point is that these two images, or ideals, have had a controlling power on civilizations, nations, periods of history, and the lives of individuals. We can understand world history and our world, he contends, by seeing the appeal and pendulum-swing of these two forces.

The Yogi image has traditionally characterized the East. The figure of the Buddha in contemplation has grasped the East for 2,500 years. The Yogi stands for a way of life which unites us with the deepest sources of creative power. Instead of being trapped and drained by the hollow, passing world, we find it is possible to gain perspective and peace. The Yogi-path leads to wisdom and self-realization.

The Commissar image has grown from Western soil, but its appeal has become worldwide. The Commissar stands for

[1] Arthur Koestler, *The Yogi and the Commissar* (New York: The Macmillan Company, 1945), pp. 3-14. The study of Koestler's disillusionment with communism and his subsequent pilgrimage can be found in *The God That Failed* (New York: Harper & Row, Publishers), ed. Richard Crossman.

the rigorous use of science and organizational planning to re-shape the world into a more productive place. Evils are man-made; man must now use the best methods available to re-form the economic and social structures of society. If force is necessary, it must be used in the interest of the greater social good.

But in our time the Yogi and the Commissar cannot be confined to East and West. The West is today ripe for the appeal of the Yogi as never before in its history. The concern of some of our most sensitive youth for Hindu insights and Zen meditation is one small indication of the new openness of the West for the Yogi-ideal.

At the same time, the traditionally Yogi-inspired East is open to the Commissar impact as never before. Smarting under the long domination of foreign Western powers, who intruded without being invited, the East has been seeking to find its true self. In order to gain perspective on the colonial period of its captivity and to organize its forces for a better tomorrow, the Marxist vision of history has proved most appealing. Also the passion for scientific and technological skills has recently characterized the East. Meditation-type people have become ardent socialists, some Communists.

Thoughtful Christians will take these images seriously as they engage in the necessary heart-searching which the times demand. Is the Christian understanding of life closer to the Yogi-ideal or the Commissar-ideal? Would a Christian exis-tence in our times be a neat blend, a careful homogenization of the two—a dash of Yogi with a strong dose of the Com-missar? Just where does the Christian church stand; or better, how does it move in the face of the pendulum-swing of the Yogi and the Commissar?

I am writing this brief study to think through the dynamics of our time in the light of the images of the Yogi and the Commissar. These images may well turn out to be over-simplifications, as most images and slogans are. These images represent the pure types, the consistent extremes; whereas most history moves in between extremes on the misty flats of mixture and compromise. Nevertheless, by isolating these two dominant strands, we may be able to see more clearly the movements of today.

But I am also seeking to use this contrast as a way of exploring again the meaning of the Christian life for today's world. This task is necessary and never ending. The formulations of an Augustine, a Luther, a Wesley, a Judson, or a Martin Luther King can be helpful as great examples. But we are still left with the task and opportunity of today's Christian adventure for us. I believe that a fresh understanding of Christian existence can come as we think of it in the light of the appeal of the Yogi and the Commissar.

My real concern is not to expound a system or chirp some glib answers. It is to engage thoughtful people in an ongoing dialogue. This is no answer-book; I hope it is a discussion starter. As I write, I am thinking of the people I meet—college students, people in the churches and in adult education classes, those attending retreats. I am thinking of those casual but fruitful conversations in restaurants, on patios, and on the street corners following a committee meeting. This little book will not greatly add to the wisdom of the experts. But I hope it will promote significant conversations about crucial matters. Are the Yogi and the Commissar the chief options in our times? Do we have to choose between them? Is the Christian life another option or a more inclusive center of integration?

2

The Lure of the Yogi

It would be possible to start at either end of the pendulum-swing. Let us begin with the Yogi. His appeal dates back to the earliest times. Far from waning, the appeal of the Yogi is increasing today throughout the world including the West as well as the East.

The impact of the life of the Buddha on millions of sensitive Asian people for 2,500 years is impressive evidence which deserves serious consideration. But the Yogi-ideal is wider than the Buddhist tradition in Asia. It has a way of recurring in the most diverse cultures and periods of history. People have a way of returning to it or rediscovering it again and again. Aldous Huxley has called it "The Perennial Philosophy." Perhaps it is the most durable philosophy because it speaks most deeply to people across cultural and time barriers.

Change, Decay, and the Abiding

Anyone can begin to understand the Yogi if he feels at all what Wordsworth meant when he wrote:

10

> The World is too much with us: late and soon,
> Getting and spending, we lay waste our powers:
> Little we see in Nature that is ours;
> We have given our hearts away, a sordid boon! [1]

"Great God," he cries, "I'd rather be a Pagan suckled in a creed outworn . . ." than to be clogged, shallow, jaded, unhearing, and insensitive to life's beauty and meaning.

The Yogi, and the Buddhist tradition in particular, has a sure instinct that we need to be saved from being clogged by the trivial. Rather than simply being swept along with the "slush of change" we need to grasp, or be grasped by, that which is significant and lasting. The Christian is closer to the Buddhist than he may realize when he sings:

> Change and decay in all around I see;
> O Thou, who changest not, abide with me. [2]

The Yogi will be the quickest to join the Hebrew historian in saying that "man does not live by bread alone . . ." (Deuteronomy 8:4, RSV). Rather he lives, if he lives really and deeply, from contact and communion with God or life's Source. The Yogi would accept as his own the Hebrew words in Deuteronomy, to live from "everything that proceeds out of the mouth of the Lord." We are meant to live from and for communication with the deepest and the best.

The Buddha, seeking enlightenment under the Bo tree, cannot be accused of wasting his time. He puts the highest priority on the things that matter most. To live with the lights on is more important than to stumble blindly. To be rooted in that which abides is more important than to be swept along gasping and fevered.

The Yogi is definitely not lazy; he demands an athletic discipline and knows from experience what Nietzsche meant when he wrote: "Believe me, friend Hollaballoo! The greatest events—are not our noisiest, but our stillest hours." [3]

[1] William Wordsworth, "The World Is Too Much with Us," *Masterpieces of Religious Verse*, ed. James D. Morrison (New York: Harper & Row, Publishers, 1948), p. 94.
[2] From the hymn "Abide with Me!"
[3] Friedrich Nietzsche, *Thus Spake Zarathustra* (New York: The Modern Library, n.d.), p. 142.

The Zen Buddhist is a this-worldly, practical person. He knows that:

> Sitting quietly, doing nothing,
> Spring comes, and the grass grows by itself.[4]

This kind of "doing nothing" may well be the most fruitful action, providing it issues in being made real by the Real, and being made whole by the Holy.

The Rhythm of Work and Meditation

The Yogi is convinced that meditation will enhance life, not diminish it. The times of quiet and vision will produce the deeper integration which is the source of more fruitful, less fragmented, work in the world.

The much loved Hindu devotional classic, the *Bhagavad-Gita*, is most explicit and very typical on this issue:

> You have the right to work, but for the work's sake only. . . . Desire for the fruits of work must never be your motive in working. . . . Perform every action with your heart fixed on the Supreme Lord. Renounce attachment to the fruits. Be even-tempered in success and failure; for it is in evenness of temper which is meant by yoga. . . .
>
> To unite the heart with Brahman (God) and then to act: that is the secret of non-attached work. In the calm of self-surrender, the seers renounce the fruits of their actions, and so reach enlightenment.[5]
>
> The world is imprisoned in its own activity, except when actions are performed as worship of God. Therefore you must perform every action sacramentally, and be free from all attachments to results.[6]

In Western Christian church history one of the most powerful, practical currents of renewal came through a group of fourteenth-century Rhinelanders known as "The Friends of God." This movement is, in many ways, one of the finest examples of a Yogi-type expression on Western soil. The most articulate spokesman of the movement was a preacher and organization man named Meister Eckhart.

In numerous sermons and lectures he sounds much like

---

[4] Quoted in Alan Watts, *The Way of Zen* (New York: Pantheon Books, Inc., 1957).

[5] *Bhagavad-Gita*, translated by Swami Prabhavananda and Christopher Isherwood (New York: New American Library Inc., 1957), Vedanta Society of Southern California, copyright holder, chapter 2.

[6] *Ibid.*, chapter 3.

the *Bhagavad-Gita* in stressing "detachment," or "disinterest." This emphasis is a basis for unattached, unfrantic activity. This style has frequently been misunderstood as a kind of cloistered retreat from the world. Actually his life, and the movement generally, was one of intense social involvement. For Eckhart "detachment" meant a refusal to get "hung up" on any particular ideas or programs. He refused to make an idol of any earthly cause. But to live in the midst of the world as a "Friend of God" meant to be free to move, work, criticize, change, and obey the Spirit's direction.[7]

In the debate as to whether Mary or Martha most fully embodied the true ideal, Eckhart voted unhesitatingly for Martha. She served her Lord with her hands and her actions; Mary *merely* sat at his feet.

These emphases of the *Bhagavad-Gita* and Meister Eckhart are typical of the best of the practical-minded Yogi.

Techniques of Realization

The Yogi has developed certain techniques which have proved helpful in leading the way to peace, perspective, and power. These have not been exactly the same in India at the time of the Buddha, China during the T'ang Dynasty, Germany in the fourteenth century, or Berkeley in the 1970's. But the amazing thing is the similarity of basic methods across the centuries and across cultures.

Almost all forms of the Yogi-style will stress three basics: a disciplined moral life as the all-important beginning; the development of methods of meditation; and growth toward maturity, understanding, or integration. In the classical Buddhist tradition, these are known as the way of morality, meditation, and wisdom. The Roman Catholic tradition has long known the way of purgation, illumination, and unification. These are the recurring stages of the Yogi's progress.

The Yogi tradition will usually include practice of the following techniques:

[7] Raymond B. Blakney, ed., *Meister Eckhart: A Modern Translation* (New York: Harper & Row, Publishers, n.d.), p. 82.

1. keeping a "quiet time"
2. regular exposure to tested scriptures which inspire
3. interaction with a group of like-minded pilgrims
4. willingness to be taught by a friend, priest, or guru
5. action in society on behalf of people, including communicative skills

The Yogi is convinced that when life crowds out these "means of grace" there is a diminishing of power and purpose. These techniques are not mechanical gimmicks, and they can be varied endlessly. They must be adapted to the person and to the situation, but something like these are "basics" to the Yogi way of life.

The clearing of the "quiet time" means that you begin to be in control of some part of the day. Wholly apart from what use you make of it, this approach is the beginning of freedom to be master, not victim, of the day's schedule.

Exposure to heart-expanding literature is a source of unparalleled enrichment. Rabindranath Tagore has expressed his gratitude for his father's habit of beginning the day with a family reading of the Hindu Upanishads. Scottish Calvinist and German Mennonite homes, among others, have known the enrichment of an exposure to the assurances of the Psalms or the paradoxes of Paul's epistles. Good reading is as important to growth as good eating and good exercise.

Group interaction is a *must* in the Yogi way; one is seldom a solitary. Others expand our horizons and correct our oddities. We grow through cross-pollination. More experienced teachers and counselors function as the succession of torchbearers; one enlightened person sets another on fire.

Communication by deeds and words is important to the Yogi-style. The Yogi complains about the inability of any words to convey the deepest experiences. But his tradition is filled with every effort to communicate by the richest use of symbols—verbal and acted. He has been the great producer of journals, letters, and books. He is called rightly the "Spiritual Counselor of Humanity." He gives himself primarily to people rather than to abstract causes.

Contemplation and Celebration

I have tried to understand the Yogi at his best. Obviously, the Yogi can be corrupt as well as creative! But at his best he is not an otherworldly escapist. He is the true celebrant. He could easily take the words of Paul for his motto:

> All that is true, all that is noble, all that is just and pure, all that is lovable and gracious, whatever is excellent and admirable—fill all your thoughts with these things (Philippians 4:8).

In his own way, and translated into many idioms, the Yogi knows what the Westminster Catechism means when it says that man's true end is to glorify God and *enjoy* him forever.

The "peak experiences" for the Yogi may seem uneventful for those whose tastes have been jaded by superficial status symbols. He will put little stock in the applause-meter, but high on his list of values will be the shared conversation, the discovery of a paragraph which *speaks,* the camaraderie of fellow strugglers, the leisure for children and the elderly, time for the teahouse and browsing in the secondhand bookstore.

These are *ends,* not means to some other end. The Yogi would respond intuitively to Abraham Heschel's fine sense for life as celebration. He writes that

> . . . the Sabbath as a day of rest, as a day of abstaining from toil, is not for the purpose of recovering one's lost strength and becoming fit for the forthcoming labor. The Sabbath is a day for the sake of life. . . .
> The Sabbath is not for the sake of weekdays; the weekdays are for the sake of Sabbath. It is not an interlude but the climax of living.[8]

The Yogi aims at a style of life which culminates in contemplation and celebration. It is easy to understand why Asian people, on the whole, have not envied the breathless, technological West. Also it is easy to understand why so much of the youth culture today finds the lure of the Yogi very compelling. There is a weariness and fatigue apparent in the West, which has seemed to the young to be hollow, impersonal, mechanical, and disintegrated. The Yogi feels he has a word, or a style, for times like these.

[8] Abraham Heschel, *The Sabbath: Its Meaning for Modern Man* (New York: Farrar, Straus & Giroux, Inc., 1951), p. 14.

3

The Logic of the Commissar

The Commissar stands at the opposite end of the pendulum-swing from the Yogi. He is not at all impressed by such themes as "inner peace," "quiet time," or "union with life's Source." To the Commissar these are empty abstractions; they divert people from the serious business of the real struggle for a better world. The Commissar believes that meditation is an escape from the problems of the world.

The Commissar in this study is a symbol for the modern man who believes that through scientific analysis and effective social planning we can increase the productivity of goods and equality of conditions now. The Commissar, here, stands for something broader than simply Communist-man. He stands for all those thoroughly this-worldly attempts to reorganize society scientifically in the interests of lifting the condition of the "have-nots." The writings of Karl Marx have become like scriptural foundations for this life-style. But the Commissar, here, symbolizes socialist and democratic experiments as well as those nations living under Communist flags.

Passion and Hope for Social Change

The Commissar sees a terrible division separating the world today. This is the division between the "haves" and the "have-nots." The group of "haves" is the smallest. They live in abundance, even affluence. They look upon others as "underdeveloped," primitive, or less fortunate. By far the largest group is the "have-nots." They live in deprived conditions with little chance to see anything better for their children or grandchildren. The population explosion will only increase the vast numbers of the "have-nots." These are the victims of a world which is divided and dominated by the "haves." But the resources of the world are vast and ample. Advances in science and technology have made it possible for *all* to share in a highly improved standard of living. The Commissar sees clearly that the basic problem is not one of the amount of resources. It is the problem of the control and distribution of resources.

When the "haves" control the wealth and the ways of getting more wealth, they can also control the resources. These resources will then be distributed in ways that will increase the wealth of the "haves." Privileged families and nations will continue to expand their wealth at the expense of the "have-nots," who will have less and less opportunity to improve their conditions. The "haves" soon assume a superiority due to their better conditions; the "have-nots" develop increasingly an inferiority mentality. Deep resentment smolders among those who refuse to accept the system which creates these divisions. This resentment can erupt and be channeled into a passion and programs for change. Revolution is the attempt to change the system for the good of the greatest numbers.

The Commissar is both pessimistic and optimistic. He is pessimistic about the possibility of the "haves" being persuaded to share with the "have-nots." To be sure, token gifts will be given sometimes, but these are often made in the interest of public relations or to salve a guilty conscience.

The Commissar knows that increased education will not alter the basic condition. Education will increase the privileges of the "haves" but never greatly alter the condition of the "have-nots." Political pressures can alter governments which organize social life, but as long as governments are controlled by those who "have," the basic structure will not be changed. The Commissar is pessimistic about more time, education, or government programs (of the kind we have) being able to alter conditions. Time is on the side of those in power.

The Commissar seeks to be utterly honest and realistic about the power struggle in today's world. Power concentrated in the hands of the few produces an elite who will cling tenaciously to their privileged position. Time will not automatically change this. *But,* the Commissar claims, *the system itself must be changed, and man can change it. Modern history has witnessed a ground swell in the direction of changing entire systems.*

The Commissar becomes boundlessly optimistic at this point. He is confident that sweeping changes are in the making. This confidence that history is on his side releases tremendous energy for working for the new day for the masses.

It is not surprising that peoples in the so-called "underdeveloped countries" respond eagerly to the good news of the prospect of better living, equality, and freedom. Peoples of Asia, Africa, and Latin America have lived through the colonial period of history. They have seen people from companies and nations of the "haves" come to their countries, exploit the natural resources and cheap labor, and better the condition of their companies and the colonial countries. But the life of the peasant has remained relatively untouched. The plight of the "have-nots" has often increased, while the privileged elite top a pyramid which includes a large slave base.

But the Commissar has brought this situation to light. He believes a change in the control and distribution of resources will bring about a new condition, a new world. When the people, meaning the majority, gain control, it will be possible to organize life in such a way that each person can contribute out of his ability and receive according to his need. Instead of exploitation, there can be equalization of opportunity. First there must come the shift of power from the privileged elite to the people. If this could come gradually, all would be well. Chances are, however, that nothing less than revolution, sometimes violent, will accomplish this. Once the revolution has taken place, the reorganization of society can follow.

We have witnessed recently the abrupt ending of colonial regimes that had seemed firmly entrenched. People throughout the world have seen that conditions can be changed. Uninvited intruders and exploiters can be removed. Robbers need not be tolerated. Force may be necessary to counter powerful robbers, but men have been discovering that force can be used to shape their destinies to more desirable ends as well.

The Commissar is the symbol of optimism in today's world, especially for those who have lived under colonial exploitation. "The people" *can* gain power and use it to reshape their world.

Justice and Revolution

The Commissar is concerned for justice and equality of opportunity. He wants "right" to prevail. He believes his constructive efforts are important in righting the present corrupt world.

But he is realistic enough to know that if a situation is to be changed, a power struggle is inevitable. The power of the new must challenge the old; the power of right and freedom must struggle against the power of injustice and exploitation. This means that revolution *of some kind* is necessary if a greater measure of justice is to prevail.

The present struggle for racial equality in America is the example nearest at hand and is typical of the problem in other areas. As early as 1932, Reinhold Niebuhr wrote in his *Moral Man and Immoral Society:*

. . . the white race in America will not admit the Negro to equal rights if it is not forced to do so. Upon that point one may speak with a dogmatism which all history justifies.[1]

But why must a relatively decent white race be *forced* to admit the Negro to equal rights? The reason lies in the fact that those in a position of privilege will bolster that position through the use of a system which will guarantee their privileges. The cries of injustice will go unheeded. Token contributions will be given as long as the system which supports the privileged can remain firm.

Niebuhr's words, like those of most prophets, were unheeded in his generation. He was considered unduly pessimistic by those who felt that education and an extension of goodwill would bridge the gap between the "haves" and the "have-nots."

The context of his words is worth pondering now, forty years later, when the revolution is upon us:

There are moral and rational forces at work for the improvement of relations between whites and Negroes. The educational advantages which have endowed Negro leaders to conduct the battle for the freedom of their race have come largely from schools established by philanthropic white people. The various inter-race commissions have performed a commendable service in eliminating misunderstandings between the races and interpreting the one to the other. But these educational and conciliatory enterprises have the limitations which all such purely rational and moral efforts reveal. They operate within a given system of injustice. The Negro schools, conducted under the auspices of white philanthropy, encourage individual Negroes to higher forms of self-realisation; but they do not make a frontal attack upon the social injustices from which the Negro suffers. . . . They do not touch his political disfranchisement or his economic disinheritance. They hope to do so in the long run, because they have the usual faith in the power of education and moral suasion to soften the heart of the white man. Thus, faith is filled with as many illusions as such expectations always are. However large the number of individual white men who do and will identify themselves completely with the Negro cause, the white race in America will not admit the Negro to equal rights if it is not forced to do so. Upon this point one might speak with a dogmatism which all history justifies. . . .

There are both spiritual and brutal elements in human life. The perennial tragedy of human history is that those who cultivate the spiritual elements usually do so by divorcing themselves from or misunderstanding the problems of collective man, where the brutal elements are most obvious. These problems therefore remain unsolved,

[1] Reinhold Niebuhr, *Moral Man and Immoral Society* (New York: Charles Scribner's Sons, 1960), p. 253.

and force clashes with force, with nothing to mitigate the brutalities or eliminate the futilities of the social struggle.[2]

The Commissar would identify with these words and underscore the line "misunderstanding the problems of collective man." The problem with the Yogi and other "spiritual" people is that they see only the isolated individual in his private quest for peace or union with God. They are blind to the problems of collective man: man in his groups, in positions of privilege or slavery, colonial power or victimized peasantry. The "spiritual" person is not vividly aware of the division of "haves" and "have-nots." He does not have vision or heart to attack and change these conditions. He is not geared to changing society for the better.

The Commissar sees that, in a society composed of groups, a power struggle between groups is inevitable. The struggle for freedom and equality implies some form of revolution.

Religion May Be Opium

The Commissar takes a dim view of religion. As long as people are consoled by the hope of "pie in the sky, by and by," they will not take seriously the plight of the downtrodden, nor will they work for better social conditions here and now.

Religion has frequently had the effect on people which is produced by the opium den. Nothing is more tranquil than an opium den. Here men recline, free from passion and anxiety, drifting along in a world apart. This opium world is created by the drug. To live in the opium world is to be unfit for the world of social struggle. Opium produces a kind of peace, but it is a peace through disengagement. It produces an unproductive tranquillity. In the end it disintegrates the person and leads him to uselessness and death.

The Commissar sees religion doing much the same to people. If he opposes religion, it is because he is concerned to see people alive and struggling for a better world. He is opposed to all that drugs and diminishes man.

[2] *Ibid.*, pp. 252-256.

As the Commissar sees life and history, he is struck by the way religion has been used by powers to maintain their position of privilege. Governments have ways of finding religion helpful in ordering society for their purposes. All the major religions have been used in this way. King Asoka vigorously spread Buddhism in India during the third century B.C. because it insured a more contented and docile people. The caste system in India has been strengthened by a traditional Hinduism. Colonial powers have included "established" or state Christian churches, which encourage a quiet life and support for the throne. Kings and priests have a way of working together to bolster each other's cause. Once they have combined forces with bankers, a formidable establishment has been formed.

The Commissar is wary of this alliance of power. It establishes the "haves" at the expense of the "have-nots." Religion then, in the Commissar's thinking, is on the side of politicians, landowners, and bankers. The revolution has to fight the power of entrenched religion, as the history of Mexico abundantly testifies.

The God of Abraham, Isaac, and Jacob—and the Commissars

The Yogi stands for contemplation; the Commissar for changing the world for the better. Are these ideals mutually exclusive? Or can they be harmonized? Is there a larger perspective which can include the best of both, while being critical of the extremes to which each is prone? These are large questions which we will seek to live with creatively, rather than dismiss with a trite formula.

But at this point it is provisionally worth noting that the vision of life stemming from the Judeo-Christian heritage *seems* to be closer to the Commissar than to the Yogi. The French scientist-philosopher of the seventeenth century, Blaise Pascal, put the contrast abruptly when he wrote: "The God of Abraham, Isaac, and Jacob, not the God of the philosophers."

God, or the Creative Force, was not to be thought of like Aristotle's Unmoved Mover, the great quiet One who sat forever contemplating perfection. This Unmoved One sat calmly on Mount Olympus far removed from the troubles and struggles of men in the world of flesh and blood. But the God made known through the Bible was one who took sides in men's struggles; he called people to cooperate with him in setting slaves free; he was forever involved in the course of history; he would roll up his sleeves and become stained in toil. He was the God of ordinary and specific people, like Abraham, Isaac, and Jacob. *He was primarily an actor not a contemplator.*

It is not surprising that Karl Marx, a Jew, can be seen as drawing heavily upon his own great tradition, for the God depicted in the Bible is concerned about men and justice, but not greatly concerned about "religion." In fact, if we can trust some of God's most authentic prophets, God frequently opposes "religion" in the name of concern for justice and equality. The words of the prophet Isaiah can be taken as typical of the best of this understanding. As spokesman for God, Isaiah says:

> New moons and sabbaths and assemblies,
> sacred seasons and ceremonies, I cannot endure.
> I cannot tolerate your new moons, and your festivals;
> they have become a burden to me,
> and I can put up with them no longer.
> When you lift your hands outspread in prayer,
> I will hide my eyes from you.
> Though you offer countless prayers,
> I will not listen.
> There is blood on your hands;
> wash yourselves and be clean.
> Put away the evil of your deeds,
> away out of my sight.
> Cease to do evil and learn to do right,
> pursue justice and champion the oppressed;
> give the orphan his rights, plead the widow's cause
> (Isaiah 1:13-17).

The Commissar sees himself as the contemporary descendant of the social prophets, Amos, Isaiah, and Jeremiah. He also knows that Jesus did not hesitate to overthrow the money changers in the temple.

The logic of the Commissar is almost irresistible. It comes

with compelling force today to the majority of the world's people. It is especially heard as a message of hope by the deprived and the exploited masses. The Commissar may not proclaim "the whole truth," but he speaks one of the most significant words in our time.

4

The Pendulum-Swing in Burma and Berkeley

We have looked at the pure types of the Yogi and the Commissar as the end points of a pendulum-swing. It will be helpful now to look at two segments of recent history in the light of the appeal of both the Yogi and the Commissar.

My selection of Burma and Berkeley, California, is purely personal. These are the places where I have lived in recent years; these are the places I know best. I believe, however, that they also represent pulsebeats of more than simply personal preference. They are representative in some sense of Southeast Asia, on the one hand, and the now-generation in America, on the other.

Burma: Pulsebeat of Southeast Asia

Burma can make a good case for being a representative Asian country. Situated strategically between India and China, its cultural history embodies elements from each of these great civilizations. The major peoples have come from central China, whereas the dominant religion, Buddhism, originated in India. The Burmese language reflects these two roots:

25

the spoken language is tonal and monosyllabic, and it is related closely to Chinese; but it utilizes a script derived from India.

The recent political history is typical of many colonial countries. A proud people were brought under the domination of an uninvited Western power, Great Britain. In 1948 Burma gained independence and began the struggle to make its own way in the modern world. The new nation has sought for roots in its own Asian past. Buddhism has been revived and sponsored by the State. At the same time, Burma has been open to Western thought and technology. Marxism has provided a helpful lens for seeing and reading Burma's recent history. After independence, technological aid was welcomed from Russia, United States, and Japan. In Burma there can be found appreciation for both the Yogi and the Commissar.

The two prime ministers of the independence period, U Nu and Ne Win, illustrate the swing of the pendulum. Particularly in U Nu the tension between both appeals can be seen clearly.

U Nu and the Buddhist Renaissance

U Nu was in many ways a combination of a Buddhist evangelist and a socialist politician. This combination made him an enigma to those who prefer their religion and politics straight and unmixed.

U Nu's early political career was closely linked with General Aung San and the secular minded nationalists, who brought an end to British colonialism and opened the new chapter of Burmese independence. But his period of political leadership, from 1950 to General Ne Win's *coup d'etat* in March, 1962, was characterized by an increasing concern for the purification and spread of Buddhism in Burma and throughout the world. In U Nu the concerns of the Yogi were dominant in a man of political responsibility.

In many ways U Nu represented a continuation of the older position of the Burmese kings with reference to the place of Buddhism in the life of the people. As prime minister, he felt that a major part of his task was to purify and strengthen the Buddhist Order of Monks (Sangha).[1] He led the way for the organization of the Sixth Great Buddhist Council, from 1954 to 1956. The chief concern of this assembly was to revive Buddhism in Asia and particularly to clarify and translate the Buddhist scriptures and commentaries. At the close of the Council, the proposal to make Buddhism the state religion was accepted as a political goal in the 1960 elections. U Nu's overwhelming victory paved the way for the constitutional amendment in August, 1961, making Buddhism officially the state religion.

U Nu believed devoutly that Burma's great contribution to a troubled world was a fresh appreciation of Buddhism. The erection of the World Peace Pagoda on the outskirts of Rangoon symbolized this concern. The dominance of the West had produced a war-filled world; the times were crying out for peace, and Buddhism was the foundation for a peaceful world. The teachings of the Buddha and especially the value of disciplined meditation were exportable and needed throughout the world. Buddhism was a universal way of life for modern man.

Buddhism was the one religion which could most easily be harmonized with the modern scientific outlook. Buddhism begins with a careful analysis of a human situation, as a doctor carefully examines a patient. There is no appeal to miracles or special revelations. The Buddhist approach leads to the acceptance of responsibility for one's life and world. In Buddhism, especially the Theravada or classical type, there is no cringing dependence on God or on an outside source of help. The person accepts responsibility and makes the most of his situation. According to U Nu, both science and socialism could be built on this foundation.

[1] Donald Smith, *Religion and Politics in Burma* (Princeton: Princeton University Press, 1965) gives a scholarly treatment of these times and issues. An introduction to the place of the Christian community in this setting can be found in my chapter, "Burma: The Church amid the Pagodas," in *Christ and Crisis in Southeast Asia* (New York: Friendship Press, Inc., 1968), edited by Gerald H. Anderson.

U Nu frequently let it be known that when he could be released from politics, he would prefer to spend his time sharing the light of the Buddha. After being released from many years of military incarceration, he again declared his intention of taking the message of the Buddha back to India, the land of its origin.

U Nu gave much time to extended periods of meditation. During the last months of his administration he was frequently criticized for spending too much time in the meditation center when the country stood in dire need of decisive leadership. From the larger Yogi perspective U Nu was not abdicating his responsibility; he was doing the most valuable thing which a leader could do in his position. As representative leader, he was keeping attuned to the deepest sources of insight and power. From this, the necessary wisdom and decisions would follow.

Ne Win and the Burmese Way to Socialism

But the pendulum swings from the Yogi to the Commissar. Practical businessmen and politicians must make immediate decisions. Efficiency cannot be sacrificed to those who meditate and dream. When the country seemed to be at a point of economic and political breakdown, the army with its rugged this-worldly efficiency stepped in to save the day.

With General Ne Win in control, the new program was called "The Burmese Way to Socialism." The accent was on the power of the people to organize their society in more productive ways. The encouragement of a pure Buddhism seemed an impossible luxury when much energy was necessary to create a sound economy and to keep Burma free from the covetous Communists and capitalists alike.

I recall a conversation which took place one evening during the time the shift was being made from U Nu to Ne Win. A government official, wholly sympathetic to the Ne Win emphasis, asked me if I planned to return to Burma after my furlough. I replied that Burma had come to be my "home" after living there for ten years; that I enjoyed my work and liked my neighbors and students; and that I surely would return if the government saw fit to allow me to reenter. I recognized that a government sponsoring Buddhism as a state religion might have real hesitations in giving reentry to a Christian missionary.

The government official immediately replied with great assurance, "Don't worry! When the Ne Win government is in power, you will have no problem. You are definitely wanted! You missionaries have built schools and hospitals and have opened agricultural stations. You have contributed greatly to the social conditions of this country. We want you." Then he added, "It is those Buddhists like U Nu who are taking our country back into the dark ages."

It was significant that he himself was a Buddhist by tradition. He had not been trained in any mission school. But as a secularized, socialist man, his concern was with freedom and efficiency. As a military man, he would not hesitate to use bulldozers or even bombs when the situation called for rapid and radical change. He represented to me the Commissar mentality reacting to the Yogi among his own countrymen.

Ne Win is a clear example of the logic of the Commissar. Social needs cry out; the socialist program and military power must move in to save and reshape the situation.

U Nu actually represented an attempt to link the Yogi and the Commissar. To be sure his accent on the Yogi called forth the subsequent Commissar reaction. But his intent was to unite a solid, renewed Buddhist base with a socialist superstructure. His ideal was to gain the best from both worlds. In this effort he bore the uneasy tension which colors much of Asian life today. The rediscovery of the authentic Asian sense for contemplation and meditation comes when the times cry out for immediate state planning, technological advance, and the use of force to change conditions.

In Burma both the lure of the Yogi and the logic of the Commissar can be seen. It is not surprising to find both at work in the same person.

Berkeley: Pulsebeat of the Now-Generation

Berkeley, California, where I now live, can be taken as a pulsebeat of today's youth scene. Once again the Yogi and the Commissar appear as distinct types; there are the "flower children" and the "new left." Berkeley is the home of both mystics and militants. The pendulum swings from Zen Buddhist meditation centers and Hare-Krishna (Hindu) chants to "People's Park," "Ho Chi Min Park," and the attempts to make Berkeley the revolutionary capital of the world.

Sensitive youth today feel the strong pull of both the Yogi and the Commissar, to the utter bewilderment of their parents. It is not surprising that they frequently oscillate between the two types, for a climate has been created which causes youth to respond to the times by either of two extremes: a meditative withdrawal from society to cultivate the intensely personal; or the passionate confrontation of the system in order to revamp it totally and now. Berkeley is the home of both types, as well as some increasing attempts to unite the extremes.

The New Mystic Quest

Nothing is more bewildering to the older generation than the mystic quest of the youth. Parents are reasonably prepared for general rebellion, atheistic outbursts, campus pranks, and a passion for materialistic prosperity. But they are at a loss to know how to converse with sons and daughters who read the *Tao Te Ching,* the *Bhagavad Gita,* and the *Tibetan Book of the Dead;* who become skilled in Yoga disciplines and enroll in Zen study centers.

A middle-aged university colleague reported recently: "My son totally resists the commuter's world of business. He insists on identifying with a small town in France in the name of simplicity and service. He is a kind of spiritual Franciscan. Imagine me having a real Franciscan in my home! We haven't been religious for three generations!"

The mystic quest is a pilgrimage toward union—union with the Source of life, with the wholeness of life, or in traditional terms, with God. The catchphrases of youth reveal the direction which they are seeking. This generation seeks to "groove with the elements"; it has an intense "merge urge." There is a passion to "be with it." The "love-in" is its symbol.

No generation in the West has devoured the ancient Chinese classic, the *Tao Te Ching,* like this youth generation. These poems call for an elemental openness and surrender to the Tao, or flowing life current that sweeps through nature and man. Fulfillment comes not in fighting or dominating nature, but in responding to and flowing with the current.

The highest priority goes to the "rap session" where one can speak and hear, where significant communication takes place. The desire is to "interact" and to get close to each other without the artificial barriers of class distinctions and intellectual concepts. At its most superficial level, this desire is a demand for "instant intimacy." But it speaks loudly the deep yearning to know and be known, to give and receive, to love and be loved.

Alan Watts has become the *guru* for this youth generation. His *The Way of Zen; Nature, Man and Woman;* and *Psychotherapy East and West,* among others, have opened up the Eastern world for Western youth. Here can be found a vision of life in its wholeness—body and spirit, both male and female, Eastern and Western, Christian and Buddhist. In contrast to over-institutional and exclusivist Western religion, he depicts a style of life which seems richer, simpler, and more real than the impoverished husks upon which the Western world has been feeding.

One of the most significant barometers of the current youth quest is the phenomenal appeal of Herman Hesse's *Siddhartha.* Probably no novel is more widely read and deeply pondered by the present student generation. In exquisite prose, which even translation cannot blunt, the German author of an earlier generation has depicted the Hindu-Buddhist quest for the realization of life's essential unity.

Siddhartha moves through the stages of life slowly discovering the One through contact with the Many.

The world of illusory values tempts toward self-exaltation, but in the end this is the way of bondage. Liberation, however, comes as the false self is stripped away and the real "selfless self" emerges, freed from craving, attachments, and goal setting; free for learning, insight, beauty, and love. Siddhartha learns that

> love is the most important thing in the world. It may be important to great thinkers to examine the world, to explain and despise it. But I think it is only important to love the world, not to despise it, not for us to hate each other, but to be able to regard the world and ourselves and all beings with love, admiration and respect.[2]

In another medium, the music of Bob Dylan reflects a pilgrimage which has "spoken" powerfully to this generation of new-mystics. His earlier songs of social protest and criticism carried an understandable load of bitterness and cynicism. But his more recent offerings, as in *John Wesley Harding,* are less concerned with political solutions. His work has become infused with a gentleness and passion which are achieved only after one is "lived through" by that Source and Love which a previous generation more easily called God.[3]

But why does this generation find the Asian mystical quest so congenial? Could it not be found in Western Christian mystical sources also? Theologian Paul Tillich once wrote that the barrenness of much Protestant Christianity was one of the contributing causes to the appeal of Zen Buddhism:

> The fact that Protestantism did not understand its relation to mysticism has produced tendencies which reject Christianity altogether for Eastern mysticism, for example, of the Zen Buddhist type. The alliance of psychoanalysis and Zen Buddhism in some members of the upper classes of Western society (those within the Protestant tradition) is a symptom of dissatisfaction with a Protestantism in which the mystical element is lost.[4]

---

[2] Herman Hesse, *Siddhartha* (New York: New Directions Publishing Corporation, © 1951), p. 119. Reprinted by permission of New Directions Publishing Corporation.

[3] Steven Goldberg, "Bob Dylan and the Poetry of Salvation," *Saturday Review,* May 30, 1970, pp. 45-46.

[4] Paul Tillich, *Systematic Theology* (Chicago: University of Chicago Press, 1963), vol. 3, p. 243.

The reasons for the new mystic quest are surely numerous. They reveal thirsts that have not been quenched. They may also reveal illusions which must be punctured. But there is no doubt about the appeal of the Yogi to the current youth generation.

The Politics of Confrontation

The Yogi is found in Berkeley, but the Commissar has far more followers. As in American history generally, the mystic is a subordinate theme to the activist. Berkeley is peculiarly the pulsebeat of the politically activist youth who are concerned to change society radically and to do it now.

The word "radical" is a key word and a good word in the vocabulary of both the youth and oppressed minorities. The Latin base of the word means "roots"; the radical is the one who goes to the root of the matter. He will not be diverted by putting salve on the skin rash when the problem is bad blood or poor circulation. He will attack the problem where the greatest change can be effected. He is interested in health, not simply in giving the impression that he is busy.

The Commissar is an appealing figure because he is concerned with the causes and cure of social disease. He is concerned with attacking "the system" which forever keeps producing the inequalities and injustices in order to perpetuate its own existence. The radical is the serious, not the superficial, person. He is not interested in trivialities or token gestures. Behind the impersonal and ineffectual educational systems, he sees again the state and capitalistic system which builds and maintains such nonproductive, authoritarian institutions. Behind the revolutions of minority people throughout the world, he sees the efforts of peoples to resist "second-class citizenship" in their own countries. Politically conscious youth of the Berkeley-type identify with the struggle of the oppressed in every land. They empathize with people seeking freedom from the tyranny of "the system," which turns out to be a combination of conservative government, military aggression, capitalist banking, and revivalist religion.

The Commissar-type youth believe that radical change is possible. Currently they are exploring every means to use the system to change the system. They believe in "participatory democracy" which means involving the power of the people to bring the needed pressures to bear on the points where significant decisions are made. Regular elections should be used, not ignored. In this way, new blood can come even into the city council. This method is currently being used to affect decisions. This generation has quickly learned the art of Power politics, a politics of confrontation. In contrast to the "lost generation" and the "apathetic generation," the Commissar has become the symbol of the "political generation."

To be sure there are frequent and sometimes violent divisions of the house on the question of tactics. When shall a demonstration be used for dramatic effect? What confrontation will have long-term educative value? What skirmishes are to be avoided in the interests of the full-scale battle? On tactical questions, discussion and compromise are always possible. The special temptation is to dogmatize concerning means as well as ends. In the heat of the battle the Commissar has not always developed skills at hearing dissent and coping with possible pluralism in his own ranks.

It is important for all to remember, especially members of the older generation, that political activism is in the American bloodstream. The country was founded in a revolution and until very recently was a hopeful symbol for peoples everywhere struggling for freedom. America led the way in the battle for independence against a colonial power.

This country became populated with immigrants seeking freedom of religion and economic opportunity. Now the children and grandchildren of the immigrants also are concerned to challenge, change, and perhaps abandon a system which sanctions injustice and exploitation. This generation has more in common with its grandparents than the beards!

This political generation stands in a long tradition of utopian politics. Fresh, experimental visions of freedom and equality challenge the slow, cumbersome, compromising establishments. Visions of a new day and a better world kindle hope and fire the imagination. But when the utopian actually achieves a place of power and responsibility, new factors compound the picture. Radicals on the city council immediately face budget limitations, competing interests, local apathy, and the need for working compromises in order to get on with the day's work. Radicals in places of responsibility become different people, because they have entered a different world. The Commissar makes a better revolutionary than an "organization man." But these experiences are still in the future for freedom seekers who now want to overhaul the entire system and not simply tinker with a few gadgets.

The Yogi and the Commissar seem to be at opposite extremes in both Burma and Berkeley. But the two pulsebeats can be found in both places. Even more—both pulsebeats can be found in the same person, for each has a word which seems to be needed. Both seem to share some basic concerns. Both the Yogi and the Commissar are concerned with a greater humanizing of life. Both are opposed to those forces which would stifle and depersonalize. Both are concerned with liberation and the fullness of life. This is why the same heart can respond to the lure of the Yogi and the logic of the Commissar.

5

The Quest for
the New Man for Today

The Yogi must be doing something right! He speaks from the earliest times with perennial appeal and freshness to the deepest in man. He can't be all wrong!

The Commissar with his vision of scientific planning also has moved the modern world in the directions of freedom and equality. He is as timely as the Yogi is timeless. Neither can be ignored!

Both of course can be perverted. The Yogi can *de*generate rather than *re*generate. "Doing his thing" may be frankly a "cop-out." The Commissar may be so sure of his analysis and program that he stops listening to the people he intends to serve. He may close discussion in his fanatical zeal. He may use power too quickly. In his desire to serve society he may be insensitive to people.

In our times it is necessary to take both the Yogi and the Commissar seriously; it is also necessary to weigh them critically. Both may have valuable partial truths, but not the whole truth. Each may need supplementation and correction, lest taken alone he obscures more than he illumines. A concern for wholeness, health, or fullness may drive us deeper than the two ends of the pendulum-swing.

Truth and the Middle Way

There is a long, solid tradition, found in both East and West, which affirms that the larger truth is not found at the extremes; the larger truth is at the center; it is a "middle path."

Gautama, the Buddha, discovered under the Bo tree that "enlightenment" and "liberation" (two terms for the same experience) were found by following the Middle Path. The extremes of religious zeal or sensuous worldliness were dead-end streets. The middle way included discipline, meditation, and the acceptance of responsibility. It moved in the direction of a freeing, mature wisdom.

The Chinese have expressed this creative center as the circle which harmonizes the richest diversity. The whole is inclusive, not exclusive. The holy would be a balanced fullness, not a partial one-sidedness. The full circle would include the Yang and the Yin, the male and the female, light and dark, strong and tender. These would not be conflicting opposites, but complementary qualities; each would help to express the other. Summer needs winter; joy needs sorrow; solitude needs society.

In hte West, Aristotle taught that the good life was achieved through the Golden Mean. Courage is the creative middle, in contrast to the extremes of cowardice (a defect) or rashness (an excess). Liberality is the healthy middle in contrast to stinginess and extravagance. A healthy modesty is "between" shamelessness and bashfulness.

When applied to the Yogi and the Commissar, this approach would imply that each might be a partial manifestation of the whole, or larger, truth. There may be a center, from which a more inclusive circle can be drawn, which includes both appreciation and criticism of the extremes. The middle way may be harder to define or describe. The end of the pendulum-swing may be a pure type that seems more consistent, less complex. But it may suffer from over-simplification. The strength of the extreme comes in part from refusing to recognize the realities attested by the other extreme.

Although our times are characterized by the extremes of the pendulum-swing, these must not obscure the deeper quest which is going on. The most sensitive in both East and West are questing for an inclusive wholeness which says "both-and" rather than quickly screaming "either-or." Harvey Cox aptly has said:

> The retreat to violence and the cop-out are similar, and they are the temptations not only of some young people but of the total society. Perhaps what our whole era needs is a vision of personal fulfillment that will not lead us to cop-out and a vision of the polis that will save us from destroying ourselves and others in our quest for human justice. Here the neomystics and the new militants need each other, and we all need them both. The only man who can save the world today must be a mixture of the saint and the revolutionary. He must be a mixture, that is, of the mystic and the militant. But how can these ingredients be combined? [1]

The Quest for a Saintly Revolutionary

The quest for a "worldly holiness" or a "holy worldliness" can be seen with unusual clarity in the life-struggle of the Italian novelist-politician, Ignazio Silone. His life and writings are a kind of seismograph upon which have been registered the shocks and issues of our generation. He is a lens through which one of the deepest quests of our time can be seen bodily.

Silone was born in 1900 in a poor, mountainous section of southern Italy. For generations, peasants had eked out a precarious existence with little help from either church or state to change their lot. As a highly sensitive boy he could not rest easily with the only two options which seemed available: to vegetate in the countryside, or to lose his soul in the bureaucratic machinery of the Fascist state.

Early in life he responded to the Franciscan version of the Christian faith which he encountered in church and school. This faith fired him with a passion to commit his life to im-

[1] Harvey Cox, *The Feast of Fools* (Cambridge, Mass.: Harvard University Press, 1969), p. 117.

proving the conditions of the people he loved. But his experience with the Catholic church in his province disillusioned him. The church seemed content to recite the rosary, say mass, recruit for the monastery, and keep peasants burdened with superstition and guilt. It did not seem to comprehend the social causes which perpetuated peasant stupor and backwardness. He was ripe for the appeal of communism. Here was a cause and a program to which he could devote all of his energies. But joining the party was no simple matter; it implied a total conversion, a new way of looking at life, the risk of losing family, social ties, and the prospect of a decent career in the established world of his time. Later he reflected:

> This explains the attraction exercised by Communism on certain categories of young men and of women, on intellectuals, and on the highly sensitive and generous people who suffer most from the wastefulness of bourgeois society. Anyone who thinks he can wean the best and most serious-minded young people away from Communism by enticing them into a well-warmed hall to play billiards, starts from an extremely limited and unintelligent conception of mankind.[2]

For many years he served the party in various underground capacities. He became a key man in the movement in Italy. But in time he became disillusioned with the cause and the whole style of life it fostered. This story is recounted vividly in his autobiographical chapter in *The God That Failed.*

The remainder of his life as artist and politician has been spent as a searcher on the "far side" of an other-worldly church and a freedom-denying, fundamentalistic communism. But in that "far country," in exile from the well-defined worlds of Catholicism or communism, he has tried to explore the territory which must become the new homeland for the new man in our times. Christian faith, as mediated through the Franciscan way, could speak powerfully to this generation. But in doing so it would mightily shake up a mummified religious institution. Socialism was a powerful vision which stood in contrast to the deadening, dogmatic bureaucracy of

---

[2] Ignazio Silone in *The God That Failed,* ed. Richard Crossman (New York: Harper & Row, Publishers, 1949), p. 99.

the Communist Party. For Silone, socialist values are permanent, while Socialist or Communist Party *policy* is very transitory indeed. The grand vision of Socialism is that of—

> a refusal to admit the existence of destiny, an extension of the ethical impulse from the restricted individual and family sphere to the whole domain of human activity, a need for effective brotherhood, an affirmation of the superiority of the human person over all the economic and social mechanisms which oppress him. As the years have gone by, there has been added to this an intuition of man's dignity and a feeling of reverence for that which in man is always trying to outdistance itself, and lies at the root of his eternal disquiet.[3]

Bread and Wine

Silone projects much of his own struggle and insight into Don Paolo, the central figure in his greatest novel, *Bread and Wine*.

The hero, a young revolutionary, dons the robe of a priest in a poor village in order to work underground. Soon he is thrust into situations of hearing confessions, giving blessings, and being sought out as a spiritual counselor. After years of abstract, revolutionary theorizing, he gains a new view of the peasant. He senses acutely the distance between the superstition and torpor of the village and the Party's slogan of "Justice and Freedom." There is little hope for change in the village and little possibility of open discussion and dialogue in the Party! Writing in his diary, he questions:

> Is it possible to take part in political life, to devote oneself to the service of the Party and remain sincere? Has not truth, for me, become Party truth? Has not justice, for me, become Party justice? Have not Party interests ended by deadening all my discrimination between moral values? Do I, too, not despise them as petty-bourgeois prejudices? Have I escaped from the opportunism of a decadent church only to fall into bondage to the opportunism of a Party? What has become of my enthusiasm of that time? By putting politics before anything else, before all other spiritual needs, have I not impoverished, sterilized my life? Has it not meant that I neglected deeper interests?[4]

[3] *Ibid.*, pp. 113-114.

[4] Ignazio Silone, *Bread and Wine* (New York: New American Library, Inc., Signet Books, 1961), pp. 68, 69. Copyright 1937 by Harper & Brothers. Copyright © 1962 by Atheneum House, Inc. Reprinted by permission of Atheneum Publishers. Silone has revised this novel, and the new edition contains a number of valuable revisions. I have quoted from the earlier edition simply because of a preference for the wording in a few passages.

One of the most dramatic encounters is his meeting with his old schoolmaster, Don Benedetto, after many years of separation. This old priest-teacher was a man at home in the classics, in his garden, and most alive when trying to arouse some fresh thinking in his students. For years Don Paolo had thought of himself as estranged from the church of which Don Benedetto was the finest symbol. Now in conversation with the old man he realizes how much of his interests and mentality have been shaped by this mind-freeing teacher. He would surely never have entered the revolutionary life without the impulse received in his religious education.

On the other hand, the religious training had made him a strange revolutionary! He could not succumb to unquestioned authority. He had tried to be a loyal Communist, but with open eyes and a questioning mind. Somehow this always got him in trouble with the Communist hierarchy; trouble very like that which Don Benedetto was always having with the church hierarchy. He never seemed capable of unquestioning obedience.

As an adult he now rediscovered his old master as a thinking, probing teacher, not as a relic of ecclesiastical obscurantism. During the conversation the old priest muses:

> In times of conspiratorial and secret struggle, the Lord is obliged to hide himself and assume pseudonyms. Besides, and you know it, He does not attach very much importance to His name; on the contrary, at the very beginning of His commandment He ordained that His name should not be taken in vain. Might not the ideal of social justice that animates the masses today be one of the pseudonyms the Lord is using to force Himself from the control of the Church and the banks?

To hear this from his old teacher was a mind-blowing experience for Don Paolo.

> The idea of God Almighty being forced to go about under a false passport amused the younger man greatly. He looked at his old schoolmaster in astonishment, and suddenly saw him in a very different light from the image of him he had preserved during the long years since they had last met. Certainly he was much nearer to him now, but the thought of the pains and torments the old man must have gone through, abandoned and alone, to reach this point saddened him and made him silent.[5]

[5] *Ibid.*, pp. 193, 194.

Much of Silone's mature reflection comes out in Don Paolo's encounter with a village girl named Christina. She stands head and shoulders above the rest in the village in terms of natural gifts, leadership ability, and capacity to understand the world. But, alas, she is soon to join the convent and become a nun. The revolutionary-priest inwardly resists the idea that her gifts and energies should not be directed to meet human needs and to change the deplorable conditions of the peasants. But what were the options beyond village stagnation, cloistered piety, and the closed, impersonal world of the Communist Party?

After seeing Christina, he would return to the quiet of his room and pour out his thoughts in his diary. Christina had justified her choice of a nun's life by saying: "In all times, in all societies, the supreme act is to give oneself to find oneself, to lose oneself to find oneself. One has only what one gives." After pondering this statement, Don Paolo writes:

Christina, it is true that one has what one gives; but how and to whom is one to give?

Our love, our disposition for sacrifice and self-abnegation are barren if dedicated to abstract and inhuman symbols; they are only fruitful if carried into relations with our fellow men. Morality can live and flourish only in practical life.

If we apply our moral feelings to the disorder that reigns about us, we cannot remain inactive and console ourselves by looking forward to another supernatural world. . . .

He is saved who frees his own spirit from the idea of resignation to the existing disorder. Spiritual life has always meant a capacity for dedication and self-sacrifice. In a society like ours a spiritual life can only be a revolutionary life. . . .

Christina, one must not be afraid, one must not be obsessed with the idea of security, even the security of one's own virtue. Spiritual life and secure life do not go together. To save oneself, one must struggle and take risks. . . .

Jumping up on tables and making speeches is not for everyone; entering a political group and struggling for the political transformation of society is not for everyone; nevertheless, a woman like you should have her eyes open to what is going on about her, and open the eyes of others who wish to keep them closed.

What a great revolution there will be in the world when persons who possess such spiritual riches as you possess, almost as a natural gift, cease expending them upon religious symbolism and devote them to the collective life. Thus a new type of saint will be born, a new type of martyr, a new type of man.[6]

[6] *Ibid.*, pp. 231-232.

The deepest quest of our times is for a new type of man: a man who is at one and the same time a saint who is involved in the social life of man; and a revolutionary who puts persons before causes, and who has not allowed political struggles to clog the springs from which the humanizing currents flow.

6
The Third-World Church

When teaching seminary students in Burma, I frequently used the images of the Yogi and the Commissar. I recall on several occasions asking if the Christian faith, or the Christian movement, is closer to the Yogi or the Commissar. Invariably the students said Christian faith is *much closer* to the Yogi. I was always left wondering if this response reflected the Buddhist background of their country or the type of Christian faith in which they had been nourished.

We have already seen that an equally good case could be made that the Christian faith is *much closer* to the Commissar.

No doubt the styles of life which come into history through Jesus Christ have affinities with *both*. Christian faith knows meditation and celebration, the rhythm of withdrawal and return, the quiet which allows communication with the Source of Life. It also knows active struggle against tyrannies in the name of more justice; it holds out hope for new eras to oppressed minorities. Christian faith has produced both its devotional mystics and its "social gospel." Churches have frequently felt the tension between prayer groups and social action groups, all serving in the name of the same Lord.

But the Christian faith does not fit *neatly* into either the Yogi or the Commissar framework. Affinities, up to a point, yes; but the differences are also important. Actually, to do justice to the Christian Way, it must be seen as a "third way" or a "third world" between the other two. ("The Way" is one of the earliest descriptions of the Christian movement, dating back to the time of our Lord. The term preserves the sense of a movement, a discipline, a style of life, and a fellowship.)

The term "Third-World" has come into prominence in recent times. It stands for those peoples and countries who do not fit easily into the opposing closed establishments. People who do not want to be dominated by Russia or the U.S.A., communism or capitalism, are third-world people. People seeking independence from one colonial power, but not wanting to be drawn under the control of another imperialistic force, are living in the Third-World.

Minorities in America, such as Blacks, Chicanos, Indians, and Asians, feel their affinities with third-world people. These have known what it is to be treated as second-class citizens in their own country. They aspire to an authentic selfhood which is not dictated by a dehumanizing structure. The youth generation feels to a large extent like a colonial people seeking freedom from established rigidity. They, too, frequently identify with third-world people and their struggles. The term "Third-World" covers a wide range of experience. Basically, it is *another* way, a way between, or a "third-force" which cannot be put in either of the other two boxes.

The Third-Race

The Christian church has, from the first, known that it was a third-force, a people-in-between, a new world which always has a way of being a Third-World.

In the Gospel of Peter (a late writing which was never fully accepted into the New Testament) we have this description of the Christian Way: " 'The way of the Greeks and the Jews is old. But you are . . . a third race.' " [1] A new world in the midst of well-defined old worlds; a new race made up of people of various races; a third-force, fresh and flexible, with a new vision and vitality—this was the character of the new way which led to the new world.

The new "Third-World in Christ" did not mean a complete repudiation of the nationality and the cultural heritage of the past. Jews brought with them their Jewishness, and Greeks brought with them the Greek heritage. These were utilized, baptized, and transformed when they became elements in the new race. But the new was a breaking-out of the confining boxes of the old. The missionary apostle Paul, who lived in the midst of this emerging third-race wrote: "When anyone is united to Christ, there is a new world; the old order has gone, and a new order has already begun" (2 Corinthians 5:17). Old elements which separated and isolated people were made subordinate. The new center (union with the Christ and the third-race) produced an enlarged, inclusive circle. To the Galatians Paul wrote:

> For through faith you are all sons of God in union with Christ Jesus. Baptized into union with him, you have all put on Christ as a garment. There is no such thing as Jew and Greek, slave and freeman, male and female; for you are all one person in Christ Jesus (Galatians 3: 26-28).

Sometimes this new third-race was described as a "new humanity" or a "new man" which the Creative Spirit (the Holy Spirit) was now fashioning out of the materials at hand. The Epistle to the Ephesians describes the breaking down of the dividing wall which kept Jew and Greek in their tight boxes. Out of the two there came the "single new humanity" —the third-race. (See Ephesians 2:11-16.)

But this new way was always being threatened by the old mentality. The old life would not die easily. It would reappear as the dominating Jewishness or Greekness. Jews tried to impose on Greeks the custom of circumcision; liberal-minded Greeks could "put-down" conservative Jews in love-

---

[1] Quoted in Ethelbert Stauffer, *New Testament Theology* (London: SCM Press Ltd., 1955), p. 45.

less condescension. The Third-World Church was always struggling to live in the midst of the two older worlds which tended toward a rigid polarization.

The struggle for the emergence of the third-race, between older, exclusive races has taken many forms. Along with Jew and Greek, the third-race has emerged between East and West, between Capitalist and Communist, between conservative and liberal. It is my growing conviction that the third-race is a way between the world of the Yogi and the Commissar. Each will bring his valuable contribution which can be utilized and baptized, but the Third-World Church will not be neatly boxed in by either of the two old worlds. For wherever the Christian community has rediscovered its youthful strength, it has found itself again as a new third-race in the midst of closed establishments.

On the Clifflike Margins, But at Home

The struggles of the Third-World in our time can throw light upon the life of the third-race. At the same time, those people who are participating in the third-race should have an immediate insight and empathy for third-world struggles everywhere.

Richard Wright, in his *White Man, Listen!* has written one of the most insightful books of our time on the psychological reactions of oppressed peoples. Significantly, he dedicates his book to:

The Westernized and Tragic Elite of Asia, Africa,
    and the West Indies—
The lonely outsiders who exist precariously on the
    clifflike margins of many cultures—men who are
distrusted, misunderstood, maligned, criticized
by Left and Right, Christian and pagan—
men who carry on their frail but indefatigable shoulders
the best of two worlds—and who,
amidst confusion and stagnation,
seek desperately for a home for their hearts;
a home which, if found,
could be a home for the hearts of all men.[2]

[2] Richard Wright, *White Man, Listen!* (Garden City, N.Y.: Doubleday & Company, Inc., Anchor Books, 1964), dedication.

In reading this, I think immediately of some of the "westernized elite" of Asia who have been my students, neighbors, and closest friends. I think of British-educated Burmese, in some ways blending the best of East and West, but frequently misunderstood by both their own countrymen and those who educated them. I think of Burmese Christians in a time of Buddhist Renaissance existing precariously on a bridge where dialogue is desperately needed and resisted from two sides. I think of Karens in Burma, like Blacks in America, the choicest of people, smarting under a sense of second-class status. I think of Eurasians in Burma, India, and Hong Kong, living on the margins of many cultures, beautiful and sensitive, but homeless and longing for rootage.

These are a "tragic elite" because conditions deny them the easy peace of those who can exist smugly in well-ordered establishments. But they are among the *avant-garde* of our times, because they "carry on their frail shoulders" the best of the two worlds. Their sensitivities and understandings have been developed through their very homelessness. They are more alive than those from left and right who criticize and malign them. But tragic as they are on the clifflike margins of many cultures, they are in deeper ways more to be envied than pitied. Homeless as they seem, they already have a vision of, and some beginning residence in, a home which is capable of being a "home for the hearts of all men."

This penetrating picture of third-world peoples could well be taken as a portrait of what the Third-World Church is meant to be. The Christian Way brings a homelessness from the old established life; "from the futile ways inherited from your fathers," as the First Epistle of Peter puts it (1 Peter 1:18, RSV). It leads to a pilgrimage in which you live in tents, as "strangers or passing travelers on earth," as the Epistle to the Hebrews puts it. (See Hebrews 11:8-16.) The security of the established cities is impossible to the pilgrim. He is, of course, always tempted to settle down; but a deeper call urges him to keep moving. Participants in this Third-World Movement, or Church, will know the loneliness of existing on the clifflike margins of many cultures. Their destiny is to be ambassadors who try to interpret the new in the face of the old. Their task is mediation and reconciliation. A sure sign of their being in the creative-middle, or third-race, is the pain of being misunderstood by both left and right. They are tempted to settle comfortably in the security of the old, but they are responding to the Creative Spirit, who says, "Behold! I am making all things new!" (Revelation 21:5).

But the homelessness of the Third-World Church is already a beginning experience of a larger home—"a home which could be a home for the hearts of all men." The Christian Way could hardly be described better than "a home for the hearts of all men." One of the most basic images for an understanding of the Christian fellowship is the shared meal. The banquet, the Lord's table, the sharing of bread and wine, is a symbol of the shared life. This home is meant for all men—a vision of The Way being universal, sometimes called catholic, ecumenical, or worldwide. From this Center the circle includes all races, types, and times.

> In Christ there is no East or West,
> In Him no South or North;
> But one great fellowship of love
> Throughout the whole wide earth.[3]

---

[3] John Oxenham's hymn, "In Christ There Is No East or West." Reprinted by permission of the American Tract Society, Oradell, New Jersey.

7
Christ:
the Center and the Circle

Those who have become members of the Third-World Church continue to live in daily contact with the old worlds, the worlds of Jew and Greek, Yogi and Commissar. They continue to share the common human experience. But they do so now from a new Center, which is the foundation of their new world. From this Center the widest possible circle can be drawn. The other worlds are understood and appreciated, even as they are critically evaluated, from the perspective of the new Center. We turn now to the nature of this Center and the circle which results from it.

Christ, the Clue to the Really Real

The Third-World Church emerges among people intimately related to Jesus Christ. These are peoples of all races and classes who are increasingly finding the Christ to be the clue to the most real and the most important in life. They have discovered that, for them, Jesus Christ is "the portrait" of the invisible God (Colossians 1:15). The Creative Spirit, which interpenetrates all of life with re-creative energy, is no vague blur. The Spirit has shown his face. Jesus Christ is "the portrait" of the Creative Spirit.

(The word "God" is meaningful to many, but increasingly an empty word to others, especially some who I hope might read this book. It freshens things up, for me, to use other words at times, especially since I believe He has no great hang-ups about names. I believe, with Ignazio Silone, that He delights to use pseudonyms and is quite willing to go about with a false passport! I like to call Him the Source of Life and the Life-Giver. I like to think of Christ as the Center, and the Spirit as the Living Christ or the Creative Spirit. If sometimes an impersonal term like Creative Energy is used, it is only to jerk us out of ruts where the familiar slides by too easily to grasp us. The Spirit, or the Center, is more he than it. But he is not one person along with other persons. The Center is like a person but more than a person. The Spirit is personal and personalizing; he makes us more richly persons. But he is not "a person." The interchanging of various terms for the Christlike God, Christ the Center, and the Creative Spirit, in these next chapters, is intentional; it is meant to be helpful. Should I fail in this, I hope you can make your own translations of terms as you go along. If so, this might prove to be one of the best rewards for reading this book. My aim is to encourage dialogue on matters of crucial importance.)

Our relationship to Christ, the Center, is *like* our relationship to an inspiring teacher or an intimate friend. The truth of Christ is like a healing, expanding relationship, not a mathematical formula. We may *know* that two plus two equal four. This knowledge can be valuable, but it can be known with a cool detachment. In contrast, *knowing Christ,* or better, being known by him, means a relationship which brings us into a new world and affects us at the very depths of our life.

Before meeting the inspiring teacher, our world was small. Actually we were hardly aware how small it was; we were quite well satisfied. But the teacher opened new worlds of ideas, interests, literature, and understanding. Once opened, our world could never be the same again. We became different. The teacher also gave us tools for a lifetime of building on our own. He had not enslaved us to his ideas and prejudices; he had freed us and equipped us for thinking and searching on our own. He was an instrument to lead to a greater maturity.

The intimate friend also brings a new and expanding world. The whole world is a different place because he, or she, has entered our circle. We look at everything with new eyes and a desire to share. We are never really alone because the friend is somehow present even when distance separates us. The friend knows us, perhaps even better than we know ourselves; but we are accepted and affirmed *in spite of* being known so thoroughly. This acceptance is a source of confidence and strength. Through the friend, we find we are at our best. In fact, we can do what we never were capable of doing before he came to us. This friendship grows with the years; we grow in and through this friendship. We will know with a quiet certainty that this friendship is the richest experience of life.

Our relationship to the Christ is *like but beyond* that relationship with the teacher or friend. It is at once humbling, expanding, freeing, strengthening, and personalizing.

We derive our picture of Jesus Christ from the pages of the Gospels in the New Testament. Through his face, or life, we see focused the face of God, or the portrait of the Creative Spirit. This becomes our finest clue to the nature of the life-giving energy which animates the universe. In fact, he creates our new world, or makes a universe, from the whirling streams of life around us.

Jesus had the piercing, realistic eye which could see to the core of a person. He could detect the phony, especially the wordy, religious phony, in a moment. This experience may not be comforting initially! But we may as well start knowing that the Christlike God is neither fooled nor kidded by us. We give ourselves away; we are known!

But Jesus showed a deep caring for people as particular individuals. He came not to expose the phony but to enable the phony to become real. This means that the Re-creative Life not only sees but also cares. His energies work in the direction of helping us grow more real, more healthy, and more useful.

Jesus identified with all types of people: rich and poor, men and women, slave and free, young and old. He had a special way of seeking out those whom the OK-World had confined to the fringes. He was accused of being a wine-bibber and a friend of prostitutes and tax collectors. This news is encouraging! It means that the Creative Spirit is no respecter of man's conventional standards. If anything, he is on the side of the hearty rather than the haughty.

Jesus had a way of reversing the usually accepted status symbols. Real living was to be measured by what we give, not what we get. Greatness consists of the capacity to serve, not the privilege of dominating with a lordly air. The capacity to receive and grow is of more significance than the status which comes from inherited privilege. This reversal of basic values means that the one who dances to the rhythm of the Spirit's movement will sooner or later run into basic conflict with the system which operates by the world's usual success symbols.

Jesus showed complete openness and acceptance of wrong-doers. They immediately realized this when they stopped covering up with phony excuses. He created an atmosphere in which honesty and new beginnings were possible. This means that our inevitable wrongdoing will not separate us from new beginnings. We can always be "re-newed." However, an attitude of judgment-on-others, and excuses-for-our-selves may condemn us to an isolated, shrunken existence.

Jesus was totally self-giving and nondefensive. In the crucial tests he did not seek for personal safety, and he did not cop out. The best government and religion of his day executed him unjustly as a common criminal. He took their action without calling for special help from heaven's angels or taking a fast boat to Rome. He endured the cross. This tells us that the heart of the universe knows suffering and pain. Even the best can be spit upon and condemned as a troublemaker. In the heart of God there is a cross.

But Jesus had an uncanny way of continuing to be present with his disciples, even after his death on the cross. He also came to be present with new disciples, as Friend and Lord. Death was not the last word! The disciples weekly celebrated the Lord's Day, or Resurrection Day. They came to be known as the Community of the Resurrection. The themes of their celebrations were "New Lives for Old," "Beyond Tragedy," "Continuous Creativity," "Victory over Sin and Death." These disciples kept making the incredible claim that "it is no longer I who live, but Christ who lives in me" (Galatians 2:20, RSV). This claim was equally strong among those who had not known Jesus physically in Palestine. This assurance means that darkness and disintegration may be real, but they do not have the last word. Beyond the worst that man can do, there is the renewing force which brings new life out of death. There is inextinguishable light which no darkness can black out.

The Third-World Church is nourished by the conviction that in seeing Jesus we have seen the Father-God (John 14:9). He inspires (in spirits) like teacher and indwells like friend. Only more! It is from this relationship to the Center that a new and expanding world is opened.

Christ and the Cosmic Process

Christ, the Center, brings a new world, including a new perspective on life and a new power to live. We have seen him as the portrait of the Creative Spirit. We now must look from another angle. We can see him as the generating Center of the whole cosmic process, as well as its highest manifestation.

Modern science has found the framework called "Emergent Evolution" useful in observing the life process as it unfolds in ever greater complexity and meaning. Rocks can be fascinating and revealing of the forces of nature, but a rose is even more mysterious and wonderful. At another level, the faithful dog who is "almost human" represents a more developed stage of complexity. But the highest in this series of life-expressions is man, combining in himself the mineral, vegetable, and animal, but in a wholly new combination. Something new has emerged in man. How fragile he is! But how highly developed are his capacities for understanding, creating, and loving.

Man not only eats fruit and excretes, but he also develops specialized menus and writes cookbooks. He also celebrates the mystery and sustaining power of life with a prayer of gratitude, turning a meal into a sacrament. He not only feels, but he also reflects and communicates his feelings in a poem or a painting. He can scream, but he also can compose a symphony and an opera. He not only piles rocks; he also builds temples. He not only lives with others; he also has an indefinite capacity to hurt, care, pout, complain, cooperate, love, and forgive.

Life can be seen as a movement from the lowest, simplest forms to the highest, most complex forms. In this process the highest will reveal the direction in which the process is tending. Man is the culmination of the process, as best we can judge. The life process would express itself most fully in the person with the most developed capacity for creative goodness. The early church father, Irenaeus, once put it: "The Glory of God is man fully alive."

In recent times the Jesuit scientist-theologian, Teilhard de Chardin, has made great use of this type of thinking, in order to make sense of the movement of life and the meaning of the Christ.[1] Combining his rich scientific background

[1] Teilhard de Chardin's works are numerous. His most important major work is *The Phenomenon of Man* (New York: Harper & Row, Publishers, 1959). But this is not the easiest place for the beginner. *How I Believe* (New York: Harper & Row, Publishers, Perennial Library PB, 1969) is a brief confessional overview. *The Divine Milieu* (New York: Harper & Row, Publishers, 1960) would be a good opening for many. *The Future of Man* (New York: Harper & Row, Publishers, 1964) is a collection of essays on many topics.

in the studies of primitive man, with his developing appreciation of Christ as the revealing Center of life, Teilhard has described Christ as the high point of the whole life process. Jesus Christ is the place where we see the unfolding process at its point of fruition. But he also is the point which exerts a kind of gravitational pull to draw life toward its fulfillment and lead it to ever higher stages. Life moves in the direction of "Christification." To grow in response to the movement of the Creative Spirit would be to grow in Christlikeness. The richest expression of life would be to be living in him, with him, through him, and for him.

Teilhard's favorite Scripture passage was Colossians 1:17 —"All things are held together in him." This "cohering in Christ" means that everything in the universe, the whole cosmic process, has an origin and a goal. The process leads in the direction of bringing "the universe . . . into a unity in Christ," as the epistle to the Ephesians puts it. (See Ephesians 1:7-10.) J. B. Phillips' translation of Teilhard's favorite Scripture puts it forcefully:

> He is both the first principle and the upholding principle of the whole scheme of creation. And now he is the head of the body which is the Church. Life from nothing began through him, and life from the dead began through him, and he is, therefore, justly called the Lord of all (Colossians 1:17-18, Phillips).

Much of the New Testament, the foundational writings for the Third-World Church, confirms this line of thought. The apostle Paul described the whole universe as groaning with the pangs of childbirth in order to bring forth its highest creation. (See Romans 8:18-25.) This highest fruition consists of sons of God who bear likeness to the Father. These children are being liberated to live as members of the family in behalf of the world.

In the epistle to the Ephesians the whole action of the Creative Spirit moves in the direction of bringing people to increasing maturity. This maturity is "measured by nothing less than the full stature of Christ." (See Ephesians 4:11-16.)

The people of the new creation, or third-race, represent the "firstfruits" of the new era. (See Romans 8:23.) These are the "down payment" of an inheritance which is still future. (See 2 Corinthians 1:22; Ephesians 1:14.) A new mutation has begun to show itself in history. It is possible to begin to participate in the "new reality" even if one is still involved in the old world. Creative tension is of the very essence of the new which is emerging in the midst of the old.

There is a profound truth behind the words of the popular song which says that it is "love that makes the world go 'round." The cosmic process is moved from the Center and in the direction of Christification—which means self-giving love. The Divine Energy moves to enable us to experience the largest measure of mature love.

But this movement is not irresistible. The deepest in man is the freedom which makes self-donation, love, and worship possible. But there is no overriding coercion in the highest reaches of man's life. There is always the possibility of self-withdrawal which closes one to the creative currents. The love which is the creative process can be resisted to the point of "dis-ease" and "dis-integration." But no amount of resistance can quench the flow of the healing, renewing cosmic process.

The Sperms of the Word Everywhere

Starting with the Christ as the Center, how then do we relate to the many worlds, cultures, religions, philosophies, and programs which appear in history? This question had to be faced as soon as the Third-World Church began to think of its relationship to Judaism and Greek philosophy. These questions have come alive in our time as East and West encounter each other in a new chapter of history. How is Christian faith related to Hinduism, Buddhism, or Communism? This concern is of one piece with the question of the Third-World Church in relationship to the Yogi and the Commissar.

In the second century a philosophy teacher named Justin was drawn into the young Third-World Church. He had proudly worn the blue philosopher's robe as a mark of his profession and his belief in the high value of the Greek philosophers. The question was, would he put off the robe now that he had found the new Center in the Christ?

He chose *not* to put off the robe. Rather, he deliberately continued to wear it as a symbol of the fact that the Christ had not made him think less of his previous profession or his Greek heritage. The new Center had placed these in a new perspective. But from the Center of Christ, a circle could be drawn which included, not excluded, the best of the past and the best of the other faiths.

This is the spirit of Edwin Markham who wrote:

> He drew a circle that shut me out—
> Heretic, rebel, a thing to flout.
> But Love and I had the wit to win:
> We drew a circle that took him in! [2]

Justin wrote:

We are taught that Christ is the first-born of God, and we have shown above that He is the reason (Word) [Logos] of whom the whole human race partake, and those who live according to reason [Word] are Christians, even though they are accounted atheists. Such were Socrates and Heraclitus among the Greeks, and those like them. . . .[3]

Justin went on to state that those who discoursed rightly saw what was kin to Christianity through the *sperms of the divine Word* which the Creative Spirit had scattered among mankind. "For all the authors were able to see the truth darkly, through the implanted seed [sperms] of reason (the Word) dwelling in them." [4] This does not mean, however, that there was no significant difference between the word scattered freely and understood in a partial way and the fullness of the Way incarnate in Jesus of Nazareth who came to be known as Jesus the Lord. Justin was concerned to see the fragmentary from the perspective of the full. He did not level the Christ down; he leveled other faiths up!

[2] Edwin Markham, "Outwitted," in *Masterpieces of Religious Verse*, ed. James D. Morrison (New York: Harper & Row, Publishers, 1948), p. 402.

[3] Justin, *Apology*, I, xlvi. 1-4, in Henry Bettenson, ed., *Documents of the Christian Church* (New York: Oxford University Press, 1963), p. 6.

[4] *Ibid., Apology*, II. xiii., p. 7.

From the perspective of Christ as the clue to the cosmic process, it is possible to assess with appreciation and balance the light found in the systems and schemes of men. If truth is found here, it has the same ultimate Source as the truth revealed through the Christ. There is no need to be defensive about labels or origins. At the same time, a principle of criticism and discrimination is introduced by viewing other faiths from the perspective of the Christ. It was the missionary apostle, Paul, who could look on the religious gropings of his time and say that God has nowhere left himself without witness. (See Acts 14:8-17.) The Creative Spirit was operative before the name of the Christ was known. But the Christ also becomes the criterion to distinguish the perversions and aberrations to which men are always prone, especially in their religious visions. Men dehumanize and depersonalize in their religions as nowhere else. The Yogi and the Commissar, as well as various forms of establishment Christianity, need the pruning knife of criticism as well as the affirming word of encouragement.

Some diagrams may help clarify this matter of the Center and the circle.

Diagram 1:

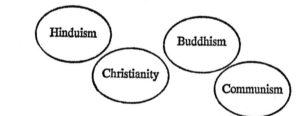

Diagram 1 may be called the billiard-ball view. Each faith is seen as a closed circle. The uniqueness of *Christianity* is affirmed, but it is found as one religion among many. It produces one ghetto among many ghettos. There is no sense here of the universality of the Christian faith. Much missionary work has been based on this closed-system approach and has never gone beyond a rigid, sectarian understanding of the faith. This version of *Christianity* has only a slight connection with the third-race or the Third-World Church.

Diagram 2:

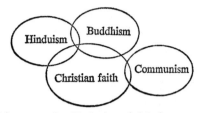

From the perspective of Diagram 2, Christian faith is seen to have its own unique Center, even as other faiths are also centered-worlds. But the Christian Way is inclusive enough to take in elements from all other faiths. The considerable overlap between the Hindu and the Buddhist ways is noted. This approach attempts to do justice to both the uniqueness and in some sense the universality of the Christian Way. But Christianity still appears as a closed system with grudging concessions to other ways. This approach is an improvement over the billiard-ball approach, but it is still lacking.

Diagram 3:

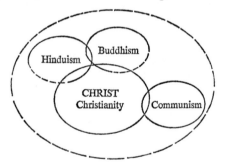

From the perspective of Diagram 3, the unique center is Jesus Christ, but the circle of inclusion is capable of indefinite expansion. It can welcome and incorporate truth however it appears. Other systems are seen as partially open and partially closed. Even Christianity, as a form of culture-religion based upon the Christ, can become a closed circle, as it frequently has in history. It must then be judged as any other closed system, both for its creative and its corrupt aspects. From this standpoint the Christ is the Center of an expanding circle which encourages *both* appreciation and criticism. These two pulsebeats are characteristic of the life-throb of the Third-World Church. There is a place for the pastor's or shepherd's heart; there is also a place for the prophet's criticism and warning.

Christ and the Contemporary Call

In seeking to interpret Christ as the Clue, the Cosmic Process, and the Center, it is possible to miss the personal, dramatic character of his call. This call has never been described better than in the moving picture sequence found in Revelation 3:20: "Behold, I stand at the door and knock; if any one hears my voice and opens the door, I will come in to him and eat with him, and he with me" (RSV). Christ takes the initiative to come, to knock, and to call. Who or what he is can be discovered only after the risk is taken to open the door. The options of an open or a closed existence are always ours. In this space of freedom, our understandings and our destinies are determined.

Albert Schweitzer concluded his scholarly *The Quest of the Historical Jesus* with these words:

> He comes to us as One unknown, without a name, as of old, by the lake-side, He came to those men who knew Him not. He speaks to us the same word: "Follow thou me!" and sets us to the tasks which He has to fulfil for our time. He commands. And to those who obey Him, whether they be wise or simple, He will reveal Himself in the toils, the conflicts, the sufferings which they shall pass through in His fellowship, and, as an ineffable mystery, they shall learn in their own experience who He is.[5]

---

[5] Albert Schweitzer, *The Quest of the Historical Jesus* (London: A. & C. Black, Ltd.; New York: The Macmillan Company, 1961), p. 403.

8

Constructive Revolutionaries

The members of the Third-World Church are called
to the tasks which the Creative Spirit is seeking to perform
in our times. Our "toils, conflicts, and sufferings" are the
ways by which we become instruments of the Spirit's struggle
to re-create the world. We are involved in nations, institutions, politics, social programs, and cultural concerns.

A generation ago, Canon Streeter wrote an essay entitled
"Christ the Constructive Revolutionary." He said:

> If I investigate the attitude of Christ towards the ideals and institutions
> of His day, I find an outlook and approach strangely appropriate to
> the present situation. Christ was no iconoclast, no lover of destruction
> for its own sake . . . but He was a revolutionary. . . . He saw clearly
> that, without drastic change, fulfilment was impossible. His interest was
> in the creative and the constructive; but He knew, and was prepared to
> pay, the price. If, then, I call Him a *constructive* revolutionary, I put
> the emphasis upon the adjective, but with no intent to weaken the
> meaning of the noun.[1]

If Jesus Christ is the portrait of the Father and the Creative Spirit, then his attitude toward the various institutions of

[1] B. H. Streeter, ed., *The Spirit* (New York: The Macmillan Company,
1919), pp. 351-352.

his day should be determinative for the style of life of the members of the third-race.

Actually Jesus embodies the tension of acceptance and criticism of institutions and programs. He could say: "Do not suppose that I have come to abolish the law and the prophets; I did not come to abolish, but to complete" (Matthew 5:17). But he could also say: "You have learned that our forefathers were told. . . . But what I tell you is this" . . . something very different (Matthew 5:21). In answer to the question of tax support for the Roman government, his statement contained the basic tension which forced all to keep thinking for themselves. "Then pay Caesar what is due to Caesar, and pay God what is due to God" (Matthew 22:21). But as soon as one separates the Roman Empire from God and gives it relative not absolute loyalty, the revolutionary potential is there.

It will come as no surprise to find the early followers of The Way accused of "turning the world upside down." What concerns us here are the reasons given for this charge against the early missionaries. "They are all acting against the decrees of Caesar, saying that there is another king, Jesus." (See Acts 17:6-7, RSV.) To live believing that "Jesus is Lord" (the earliest creed of the church)[2] meant to treat every earthly government or ruler as a fallible, human institution. Being human did not mean that the ruler was undeserving of loyalty and respect, but it did mean that human leadership was always subject to criticism; it was not God, not the Center from which life proceeded.

Third-World Christians were creative when this tension was kept alive, but maintaining the tension was a costly business. The apostle Paul urged the Christians at Rome to cooperate with the government "for they are God's agents working for your good." (See Romans 13:1-7.) But submission to human government was not an absolute. When necessary the same people stood before administrators of either church or state and said, "We must obey God rather than men" (Acts 5:29).

[2] See Philippians 2:11; Romans 10:9-10; 1 Corinthians 12:2-3.

Total commitment to "Our Lord the Spirit," as the Center, leaves one free to cooperate with or criticize the institutions and programs of our world. In fact, it commits one to perpetual examination. The Third-World Church believes with Plato that "the unexamined life is not worth living." This is one of the reasons why commitment to the Center of Life produces persons who are "fully alive."

The Third-World Church Among Third-World Peoples

There is a "missionary myth" which suggests that all is well and thriving "over there" especially among primitive peoples. In the churches here, things are dull, but money invested in the cause "over there" pays rich dividends. Fortunately, this illusion is being punctured; eventually the cause of the Christian mission will be strengthened by a more honest and realistic view.

But we follow a sound instinct if we assume that whenever the Third-World Church takes strong roots among a third-world people something explosive is about to happen. There will also be something in these situations of immense educational value, especially for those of the Third-World Church who also live within the establishment of the first two worlds!

I recall vividly a conversation one evening at dinner on a British boat on our way to Burma for the first time in 1952. The chief engineer of the ship was an exemplary Englishman who had spent a lifetime on such voyages. He had met many missionaries over the years and had followed with concern the history of colonial politics. He expressed a most sincere desire that somehow missionaries would not "stir up the hill peoples." They had lived such simple, beautiful lives until the coming of the missionary had made them restless. Now in many countries the hill peoples were involved in insurrections and civil wars, as the result of a Christian education.

The chief engineer may have been unduly romantic about the simple, beautiful life of the hill peoples. Chances are he was dominated by "the myth of the happy savage." If his knowledge of history had been better, he would also have known that the restlessness of many of the peoples dated back to a second-class status in their own land, long before the coming of the Christian missionary. But he was surely right in realizing that a Christian education, when it really takes, carries with it the seeds of revolutionary impulse.

A people awakened and growing are bound to act. When formerly oppressed people begin to realize their true potential, the reason for the conditions obtaining, and the chances of bringing changes, there is bound to be ferment. Whether this vision can be constructively channeled or will end in disruption and frustration, will depend upon the leadership's capacity for the art of politics and education.

In Burma, the largest minority people are the Karens. They are numerically to the majority Burmese about like blacks are to whites in America. The Christian movement has taken firm root among these amazing people. Naturally self-reliant, they have built their own schools, hospitals, and agricultural stations. Largely through their contacts with the Christian faith they have discovered their own selfhood. When they began their insurrection against the ruling Burmese in 1949, this was reported in American papers as "Baptist Rebellion in Burma." By the time I arrived, the Karens were smarting under the loss of the civil war, and they hardly knew where to turn or how to operate politically. In a sense, they had been "put in their place," and they definitely did not like "their place."

The questions on the minds of their youth were: Is it right to use force to gain justice when peaceful methods have fallen on deaf ears? How long do you remain passive, and when do you do something about the situation? What methods are constructive and justified?

The similarity between those questions and the ones now asked in the black community in the United States will be readily apparent.

It is no accident that the Third-World Church, through the modern missionary movement, has had its most fruitful response among minority peoples—peoples ripe for a new beginning, a new world. The Christian community is to be found in great strength among Nagas in India, Karens and Kachins in Burma, Bataks in Indonesia, and similarly among many of the African peoples. These situations have proved "ripe for the gospel" and also ripe for revolution. Frequently Western Christians, with a non-revolutionary understanding of their faith, have been dumbfounded when the revolutionary gospel was taken seriously by third-world peoples.

Very likely we are only in the *beginning stages* of constructive thought about revolutions and politics. The sons and daughters of the American Revolution are just beginning to struggle with the complexities of several simultaneous revolutions. My point here is to simply indicate that the Third-World Church has a way of producing a revolutionary people.

Revolutionaries: Not Wild-Eyed, But Open-Eyed

The Third-World Church produces revolutionaries. But they are not *ordinary* revolutionaries; they are a strange breed. The idea of a *constructive* revolutionary represents the new element.

Ignazio Silone tells of one evening when a group of Italian Communists met to plan strategy.[3] A painter in the group explained that while he had staked his life on the revolution, he insisted on the right to keep his eyes open. The other party members looked at him with considerable suspicion. The painter assured them that he would do anything expected of him, but that he just wanted to keep his eyes open, which by implication meant to be free to keep raising questions.

This unwillingness to totally commit oneself to a closed, total system is what marks the watershed between a fanatical and a constructive revolutionary. To put it in another way: the capacity to be self-critical means a built-in check on the wild-eyed revolutionary; it makes possible the strange, constructive revolutionary. But this is the rarest of gifts! Christian thought has followed a true instinct in affirming that

[3] Ignazio Silone in *The God That Failed*, ed. Richard Crossman (New York: Harper & Row, Publishers, 1949), pp. 78f.

repentance is not so much a human achievement as it is an evidence of the work of the Creative Spirit working through the human spirit.

Robert Bellah, the University of California sociologist, has given us a glimpse of his own pilgrimage in the autobiographical introduction to his recent collection of essays, *Beyond Belief*. After taking Marxism seriously in his student days, he began to be open to a number of other currents. He writes:

It was in this situation that the new attitude toward Christianity which I had been developing with the help of Paul Tillich came to a kind of fruition. It was then that I understood existentially the Christian doctrine of sin. I saw that the worst is only a hair's breadth away from the best in any man and any society. *I saw that unbroken commitment to any individual or any group is bound to be demonic. Nothing human can bear such a weight. The totalism of Communism and the totalism of the "Free World" are equally destructive.* [Italics mine.] And I learned to see the darkness within, that we are all assassins in our hearts. If I am not a murderer it is because of the grace I have received through the love and support of others, not through the lack of murderous impulses within me. The only difference between me and the man on death row is that he somehow received less grace. Feeling all this I could no longer hate, or rather justify hatred. Since I participate in the guilt of every man there is no man I can reject or declare unforgivable. This is what the New Testament taught me in those months contradicting culture Christianity and Marxism, both of which make idolatrous commitments to particular structures and persons and foster a consequent self-righteousness. It was then that I saw that identification with the body of Christ meant identification with all men without exception.[4]

This is the solid foundation for the life of the constructive revolutionary. Identification with the body of Christ links one at the same time to all men. When we see ourselves in solidarity with all men—all who build and blend into totalisms and who cop out when the going is rough—we will see that pots need not call kettles black. This perspective cuts the nerve of self-righteousness. We are then free to take men, movements, and institutions seriously, without taking them idolatrously.

The constructive revolutionary does not shout so loudly, but he has his eyes open. He moves more cautiously than the

[4] Robert N. Bellah, *Beyond Belief* (New York: Harper & Row, Publishers, 1970), pp. xv, xvi.

destructive revolutionary, but the ground he gains is more solid ground. He is more concerned with persons than abstract causes.

In the face of the hard problems, the *de*structive revolutionary quickly cuts the knot. In contrast, the *con*structive revolutionary patiently works to untie the rope.

There are good reasons for this. The constructive revolutionary has a high view of people, bodies, groups, and histories. All of these are concrete. He takes their concreteness seriously. He can take time, consider people, and reshape groups. He has come to believe that the Creative Spirit works through concrete human realities. Flying off in impatience is the way of the cop-out. This is *not* the way the Creative Spirit works. In his highest manifestations the Spirit indwells a body —Jesus Christ; and he calls a group of imperfect people into his body—the church. Since this is so, the revolutionaries of the Third-World Church are marked by a capacity to "hangin" when others "drop out." This thin line marks the difference between iconoclastic revolutionaries and constructive revolutionaries.

Will You Sing Hymns or Encourage Revolutions?

A few years ago in Burma I was asked to preach at a large association meeting held by Karen Christians. The gathering (of over five thousand people) was to be held in a village in the Irrawaddy Delta where the Karen insurrection had been fiercely fought just a few years before.

Since the government was still taking routine precautions, it was necessary for me to secure a travel permit from the police in Bassein before heading out for the village. I recall the police officer as a typical, friendly, extrovert Burman. Though a Buddhist, he might well have been educated in a mission school. I recall his genuine kindness to me as he made his routine inspection.

After a number of preliminary questions he poised his pencil in readiness to check off my name. Before doing so he asked casually, "Dr. Clasper, you aren't going in there to stir up any political trouble, are you? All you are going to do is to spend a few days singing hymns, saying prayers, and preaching long sermons, right? You really aren't going to *do* anything while you are there, are you?"

I had a hard time knowing how to respond to this. There was no doubt that he was *for* me and was simply carrying out a routine job. But to say that I wasn't going to *do* anything was too much. I would hesitate to imply that I was perfectly innocuous, that I was a member of an order which went to the other side of the world just because our kind were fond of hymn-singing and prayer-saying. But how would he have understood me and what good would have been served by telling him that I was an authorized agent of the most revolutionary body in the world! The movement of which I was a part had challenged and outlasted the Roman Empire and numerous other empires. I was going to the meeting to report on the state of revolutions now going on throughout the world and to encourage these Karens to play their part in the struggle at hand.

If I had said that, my meaning would not likely have been understood; and I surely would not have had permission to attend the meeting.

But how should we respond to that question? Perhaps this is a parable of the situation as it confronts the members of the Third-World Church today. We want to be yeasty people in the tradition of those accused at Thessalonica of "turning the world upside down." At the same time we want to be "instruments of His peace," the cement that helps hold broken situations together. The call to be constructive revolutionaries is a call to face the new and untried as an instrument of the Creative Spirit.

9

Continuous Reformation

The participant in the Third-World Church relates to the social and political institutions of his time as a constructive revolutionary. But he must also relate to an inevitable institutionalizing of the *movement* of the Third-World Church. The movement of the Third-World Church is always prior to, and more important than, the many forms through which its life is expressed. The movement *must* take shape bodily. But in time the bodies—organizations, theologies, ways of worship, styles of life—can clog the movement. This tendency calls for reforming the bodies, or institutions, so that adequate expression can be given to the movement.

In the face of the institutionalization of the Third-World Church, we discover that we must be forever engaged in continuous reformation.

Movements of the Spirit have sometimes followed a process similar to that associated with the amassing of great wealth. The first generation *accumulates* wealth through hard work; the second generation *conserves* it; the third generation takes it for granted and begins to *squander* it. By the fourth generation a new start must be made, and the cycle starts over.

Movements of fresh vitality in the religious world in general, and in the Third-World Church in particular, often unfold in a similar pattern. The Protestant Reformation, the Wesley Revival, and the so-called "modern missionary movement" reveal a similar logic. Take the modern missionary movement as an example. Frequently, the first generation Christians pay a high price to break with old environments and become part of a new, pioneer movement in their conservative countries. These "converts" make up in zeal and enthusiasm what they lack in roots and balance. The second generation has the benefit of a better education. They make good trustees of institutions. They are symbolized by the sane organization man. The third generation is in a slippery place. Much of the old heritage has "not taken," or at least it no longer *speaks* to the new questions and problems. Whether to maintain sentimental attachment or break completely is the dilemma of the third generation. Here some new beginning must appear, or the heritage will be dissolved.

Many members of the Third-World Church will find themselves today accurately described in terms of the slippery place of the third generation. This situation is true in the West, where earlier revival movements have given birth to the present form of the movement. But it is also true in the East, where the modern missionary movement has given the form to the present Third-World Church. Hence, we look with special concern to members of the so-called "younger churches." *They are the Third-World Church among third-world people in the crucial third generation!*

But all of us, whether in East or West, live at a time when new reformation is necessary. As Pope John said a few years ago, we need to open up the windows and let in a breath of fresh air. These words are powerfully symbolic. The breath of air is the Creative Spirit, who freshens and invigorates; but opening the windows is our responsibility. To participate in the Third-World Church means to be called to participate in continuous reformation.

Treasure in Earthenware Pots

As an aid to continuous reformation, we need to be clear about one of the most important distinctions: the treasure is conveyed in earthenware pots, but the pots are not the treasure.

This distinction is taken from the early literature of the Third-World Church. The apostle Paul uses it in his second letter to the Corinthians. He states that the Source of all Life —the Creator God—who first caused light to break into the darkness, has caused light to break into our darkened lives. This light, which comes as renewing, creative energy, is called "God's glory," and it has a face—the face of Jesus Christ. (See 2 Corinthians 4:3-7.)

This possibility of people now sharing in the new creation, the new era, is what is called the "Good News" or "the gospel." This possibility is what the new people, the third-race, are to communicate to the world. But this Good News, the treasure, is conveyed in very fragile earthenware pots. It is conveyed by very ordinary people with problems and complexes, using words and expressions current at the time and working together in organizations which show all of the marks of divisions and strife. This Good News could not be bodied forth without bodies, or instruments. But the earthenware instruments are definitely dated. They show the marks of time and place. They are disposable; there is no great glory in them. But they are necessary; their greatness consists in their usefulness in transmitting the treasure.

This treasure of inexhaustible potency has been conveyed by earthenware pots—people and organizations—marked "made in Italy," "made in U.S.A.," and "made in Japan." The Good News has been communicated with German accents, as well as Scottish and Burmese. The earthenware pots have been dated 480, 1640, and 1920.

In the matter of continuous reformation we need to realize that the earthenware pots are to be used, not worshiped. When they are no longer useful, other earthenware pots are to be fashioned and put to use. Concretely, this means that the church organizations, theologies, and forms of mission, ministry, and worship are dated, disposable pots. *The treasure cannot be conveyed without them; but they are not the treasure.* When they are no longer useful, new conveyors are needed. It is this reshaping of useful pots that we call "continuous reformation" in the Third-World Church.

One Gospel—Many Theologies

There is one central element in the Good News: "God was in Christ reconciling the world to himself" (2 Corinthians 5:19). Or we may express it: The Word (Logos) became flesh and came to dwell among us. (See John 1:14.) Or we may put it simply: "God is love" (1 John 4:16). Actually, "it" can be put in a thousand ways, and already the New Testament has been translated into well over a thousand languages. As soon as we select and arrange words to "body forth" the Good News, we are involved in theology. There may be good theology or bad theology, useful or unuseful theology. But being human, some words must be used. This makes the theological task necessary.

The poet Tennyson put the distinction between gospel and theology well when he wrote:

> Our little systems have their day;
> They have their day and cease to be;
> They are but broken lights of thee,
> And thou, O Lord art more than they.[1]

Great "systems" of theology are associated with the names of Augustine, Luther, Calvin, Wesley, and Barth. These and many more modest efforts have been helpful instruments for conveying the Good News to their own generations. These efforts have helped innumerable interpreters to fashion their own sermons and teaching. But they are at best earthenware pots, showing by their construction the time and place of their making. Never are they to be worshiped. When they cease being useful, they need not be retained.

[1] Alfred, Lord Tennyson, "Strong Son of God," in *In Memoriam A.H.H.*

Theology must always be redone, which means reformed. Theology is meant to be contemporary; that is, the Good News is to be put into the language of contemporary man so he can hear and respond to it. Using yesterday's language or a foreign tongue may stop the communication process. This is why the "Faith of Our Fathers" must be reappropriated and put into our own language if it is to have significance for us and the possibility of communication.

Sam Walter Foss put it well:

> So we make our catechism; but our work is never done—
> For a father's catechism never fits a father's son.[2]

Interestingly, sons come to appreciate their parents most when they face their own responsibilities in their generation. Older theologies can be appreciated most when seen as earlier attempts to communicate with *their* world. They may even become *models* of good work. But they can never be *substitutes* for doing our work today. The one gospel always needs fresh theological expression.

One Church—Many Churches

There is only one "body of Christ," or church. If we are "in Christ," engrafted into the Source-Center, we are members of that body along with other members. But our entrance and access to the one church will be through one of many possible doors. These doors represent different groups and traditions. They are datable, like earthenware pots, and they are disposable.

The one church has, from the earliest days, been described by "the Marks of the Church." These are not so many descriptions of what churches now are, as directions in which they are called to move. The church is *one;* there are not several bodies of Christ. In belonging to the Christ, we belong to each other. The church is *holy;* this is the unique meeting point of the divine-human encounter. The church is *apostolic;*

[2] S. W. Foss, "The Higher Catechism," in *The World's Great Religious Poetry,* ed. Caroline Hill (New York: The Macmillan Company, 1923), p. 74.

it is commissioned to share the Good News. Its business is communication. The church is *catholic;* it exists for the *world;* and it is to be inclusive of the *whole* world.

But our participation in the one church is dependent upon contact with one of the doors or churches. These doors may be marked Roman Catholic, Presbyterian, Baptist, or by hundreds of names. These doors may show the architecture of England, Zaire, Chile, or Thailand. The culture of these local churches may reveal incense, organs, drums, accordions, or rock bands.

The churches are temporary. The traditions come and go. Some have amazing endurance. Some hang on when they have outlived their usefulness. Some are more like museums than "meeting places" where the Lord of Life is encountered, heard, and obeyed.

The Creative Spirit is not confined to groups which call themselves churches. Like the wind, the Spirit has free movement. But history shows that we seldom, if ever, experience the one church if we ignore or despise the earthenware pots called the churches. Participants in the Third-World Church are involved in the reshaping of the local churches.

One Mission—Many Missions

There is one mission, and it is called the "Great Commission." "Go forth to every part of the world, and proclaim the Good News to the whole creation" (Mark 16:15; see also Matthew 28:16-20). But the sharing of the Good News takes many forms. These forms of communication are the various missions. These forms always stand in need of "re-forming."

These missions, like the groups and traditions, are dated, earthenware pots, in which the treasure is conveyed. Some are marked Moravian Missions in U.S.A., eighteenth century; Jesuits in China, seventeenth century; Franciscans in California, nineteenth century; Baptists in Burma; Methodists in India. Some missions communicate through schools and hospitals; others through printing presses and radio stations. Communication takes place not only through words, but through relief to famine areas and through the teaching of agricultural techniques in farming communities.

Sometimes people become attached to *missions* in such a way that they cannot conceive of the mission without one special form. Missions in our era have frequently been associated with white foreigners establishing Western-style schools, hospitals, and churches in countries occupied by Western colonial powers. When these countries struggle for independence and force the colonial rulers to go home, an entirely new situation prevails. New forms of missions are needed in newly independent countries today. This new situation calls for imagination, experimentation, and adaptability. The one mission depends upon the continuous reforming of the many missions.

One Spirit—Many Ministries

The epistle to the Ephesians describes the one Spirit, whom we have called the Creative Spirit, giving diverse gifts to peoples and groups in the Third-World Church. These gifts are varied, but the one aim is "to equip God's people for work in his service, to the building up of the body of Christ" (Ephesians 4:12). These gifts are to help build a people in unity and maturity, a maturity measured by the fullness of life as seen in Jesus Christ. The Spirit's work is not vague and incomprehensible. He moves in specific ways and with definite ends in view.

These early gifts for ministry were listed as "some to be apostles, some prophets, some evangelists, some pastors and teachers . . ." (Ephesians 4:11).

Since the Creative Spirit is no less operative today than two thousand years ago, it is safe to assume that gifts are similarly given today for the upbuilding of the serving community in unity and maturity. The question is, are these gifts received, recognized, and used?

The specific forms of ministry are as dated as earthenware pots. Evangelists in first-century Palestine performed differently than English evangelists in the eighteenth century or

American evangelists in the twentieth century. Pastors' roles have changed in various countries and times. Apostles were seen both with and without wives in the early church! Discussions continue today whether one condition is preferable or mandatory for today's apostles. Ministries have involved both "full-time clergy" and the "lay apostolate."

In all of this there is an unchanging Creative Spirit, which is expressed in a timely manifestation. Continuous reforming means an openness to the Spirit's contemporary expression. Yesterday's yardsticks may be useless in charting today's movements.

One Worship—Many Liturgies

The adoration of Our Lord the Spirit expresses itself in self-donation to be instruments of his peace. Worship is an end, not a means. We are made to respond to and reflect the "glory" or the creative love of the Creative Spirit. True worship of God involves creative service for man.

But worshiping God "in spirit and in truth" is nurtured and expressed through various forms. In the process of life, old symbols lose their force and change with new stages of life. Nothing can be more deadening than a continual use of religious forms which are no longer a living part of the people. This is why the reforming of liturgies must be a continuous process.

In our days, liturgical renewal has been experienced by many segments of the Third-World Church. Sometimes this renewal has meant a re-learning of modes long forgotten. This has called for rediscovery and education. At other times it has meant experimentation in using contemporary materials and expressions taken from the daily secular world. Some musicians inform us that the reformation and experimentation in music in the churches is second only to that period of renewal known as the Protestant Reformation in the sixteenth century.

Different traditions are able to learn from each other, so that new forms develop through new encounters. Roman

Catholics have discovered new life and meaning through the use of the vernacular languages (English in the United States) in their liturgy, rather than Latin. Bible study groups have been rediscovered as a fresh approach in the Roman Catholic tradition. Episcopalian and Lutheran churches have been among the most experimental in using rock music. This usage is significant since, previously, their liturgies were among the most "fixed" in Protestant groups. Baptists, often solidly rooted in the gospel-song tradition, have begun to appreciate Bach's music and Rembrandt's painting.

It may well be that in the reforming of liturgies we shall come to appreciate the value of *both* the cathedral and the chapel. As old sectarian walls of denominational boxes are broken down, there is an increasing urge to experience worship with the whole of the Third-World Church in any one place. Such worship means a gathering of all within the house of God regardless of which tradition's door happened to be used for entrance. The worship in the cathedral is "common worship"; that is, the central, basic elements which all have in common are used. This worship will be more traditional and less experimental.

But the chapel, or the *ad hoc* special interest group, will also have a place. Here like-minded people with peculiar tastes and interests can follow them without having first to get the sanction of the whole people. Special concerns can be given immediate priority. These need not be divisive of the whole group or of interest to everyone. These are cells which can form and reform in the interests of doing an immediate task or bearing a particular concern. But these small groups will be at their best when they are a supplement, not a substitute, for common worship.

Roman Catholics, freshly energized by liturgical renewal in their groups, soon discovered that the people most concerned about reforming worship were the same ones concerned about being constructive revolutionaries in social causes. This was no accident. To be aroused from lethargy means to be awake for many concerns. Whereas, sensing no need for continuous reformation is likely to be of one piece with falling back from the demanding third-race into the dubious safety of a closed, stagnant world. Participation in the Third-World Church is a call to an expanding and risk-taking life. This life is open-ended; it calls for people to be open-minded, ready to be flutes through which the breath of the Spirit blows new music.

The Five Deaths of the Faith

G. K. Chesterton once wrote of "the five deaths of the faith."[3] He noted that at five periods of crisis in history "Christianity" died. This death was not from external persecution; persecution usually had the effect of reducing over-weight and fanning sparks into flames. But death came when plausible oversimplifications took over and emasculated the virility of the faith.

At least five times, therefore, with the Arian and the Albigensian, with the Humanist skeptic, after Voltaire and after Darwin, the Faith has to all appearance gone to the dogs. In each of these five cases it was the dog that died.[4]

But the surprising fact is that at every turn the faith experienced resurrection. "Christianity has died many times and risen again; for it had a god who knew the way out of the grave."[5] Just when it all seemed to be over, fresh theology, new experiments, new life-styles, and adventurers marked a fresh appropriation of the one gospel, and the one renewing Spirit.

It would seem that times of severe crisis and testing are the peculiarly appropriate times when the Creative Spirit can break in to do his new thing. When the old is breaking up and coming unglued, there is an openness which makes possible renovation and reforming. Therefore, the present time is very crucial for the life of the Third-World Church. The timid may fear the storm, but the more adventurous

---

[3] G. K. Chesterton, *The Everlasting Man* (New York: Dodd, Mead & Company, 1925), pp. 312 ff.

[4] *Ibid.*, pp. 319-320.

[5] *Ibid.*, p. 312.

know that a time of new reformation is upon us. The big question is whether we will settle for jobs as custodians of musty museums or become craftsmen seeking to re-fashion churches, theologies, missions, ministries, and liturgies. What we fashion will be, at best, frail earthenware pots. These will be stamped by our time and place, but in their own way they will be useful instruments. Through them the Good News, the Renewing Spirit, and the reborn people will live in our time.

The Third-World Church has less reason than other groups to fear change. It has no reason to clutch nostalgically at that which is decaying. Deriving its life from the Center means that it can learn readily from the past, but its face is turned to the future. Herbert Butterfield, the British historian, closes his fine study of *Christianity and History* with these words:

> In these days also when people are so much the prisoners of systems—especially the prisoners of those general ideas which mark the spirit of the age—it is not always realised that belief in God gives us greater elasticity of mind. . . . Christians have too often tried to put the brake on things in the past, but at the critical turning-points in history they have less reason than others to be afraid that a new kind of society or civilisation will leave them with nothing to live for. . . . We can do worse than remember a principle which both gives us a firm Rock and leaves us the maximum elasticity for our minds: the principle: Hold to Christ, and for the rest be totally uncommitted.[6]

Being *uncommitted* to closed systems and outmoded institutions carries with it the responsibility of being *constructive* revolutionaries who are engaged in *continuous* reformation. It is our holding to Christ—or better—our being grasped by him, which makes this open life possible.

[6] Herbert Butterfield, *Christianity and History* (New York: Charles Scribner's Sons, 1950), pp. 145-146.

10 ▓▓▓▓
▓▓▓▓▓▓▓The Life of the Ambassador

Holderlin, the German poet, has somewhere said, "Poetically doth man dwell." I gather he means that man does not live by bread alone; he lives in the light of, and by the power of, certain dominant images.

We have seen that the Yogi and the Commissar are two dominant images of our time. Along with these, we have set another cluster of images: the third-race; Christ as the portrait of the Creative Spirit; and the people of The Way, who are characterized as constructive revolutionaries in the world and engaged in continuous reformation within their own special community. I now want to gather together this cluster of images into one master-image. Along with the lure of the Yogi and the logic of the Commissar I want to examine the life of the Ambassador.

The Master-Image for our Times

Certain images have a way of speaking to the special conditions of a people or period. This characteristic is true of the world in general and equally true of the life of the Third-

World Church. In the early church the image of the sacrament as "the medicine of immortality" carried great force, although it probably strikes us as strange today. At the time of the Protestant Reformation, the phrase "justification by faith alone" spoke to and for the period in a unique way. Modern Protestants of one type at one stage were especially grasped by the figure of "following Jesus."

Certain images of the church have proved especially useful at certain times. The church as Christ's Bride was especially meaningful in the twelfth century at the time of St. Bernard. For a long period the figure of the church as Christ's Body almost controlled thinking about the nature of the church. In recent days of renewal the figure of the church as God's Pilgrim People has seemed a more dynamic and less static image. This image has helped focus the need for growth and change.

Images for the "new man" have also reflected the special circumstances of the times. These are, of course, drawn from the New Testament, which is a kind of stockpile of images. But which one happens to emerge and especially "speak" is part of the unpredictable mystery of history. No one can summon an image and be sure that it will "click." The images of God's Servants, God's Children, Christ's Disciples, and Christian Soldiers have all had their special and limited usefulness.

I am suggesting that perhaps the master-image for our time could be "Ambassadors for Christ." This image is to be found in the classic paragraph from Paul's letter to which we have already referred, 2 Corinthians 5:17-20. This passage is the climax of a cluster of images, which are central to an understanding of the New Testament and especially meaningful in our times. Being organically linked with the Center (Christ) means the opening of a new world. The old era begins to fade, and the new age emerges. The Divine Energy moves to this end, and the people of the new age are used as instruments in this re-creative, renewing process. New people are the bearers of the Good News. Then comes the climax: "We come therefore as Christ's ambassadors."

The life of the Ambassador for Christ embodies the purpose of the Third-World Church. The ambassador lives "between." He is a commissioned person. He is sent on a mission representing the new era and the new world in the midst of old times and old worlds. In representing the new, he makes it present; that is, he is the *embodiment* of the new order.

His service is primarily one of communication. He must be skilled in at least two languages: the language of the community which commissions him, and the language of the people with whom he lives. As a communicator he must be skilled in the art of listening and learning as well as in speaking and interpreting. The primary skills of the ambassador are understanding, mediation, and reconciliation. He is not primarily a solo performer. He is the representative of one community in the midst of other communities.

Divinely Intended Tensions

Tension is the essence of the ambassador's life. Growth for him means increased capacity to endure tension and to use it constructively. Baron Von Hugel was fond of saying that some tensions are disintegrating; but there are also "divinely intended tensions." The ambassador's life embodies these.

Each decade I have lived has seemed at the time the most interesting! Currently I am enjoying the "fascinating forties." During the middle years the spread of contacts is at its widest (I am told). At this period our children are trying to keep us young, and we are still in touch with our parents. But being in the middle is sometimes a strange and strained existence. Our world is not the world of our parents; but the youth remind us that our world is not theirs either. It is quite possible to be rejected from two sides at once—reminiscent of Richard Wright's "distrusted, misunderstood, maligned, criticized, by Left and Right. . . ." In the middle years there is a built-in tension; there is no escaping it. Nevertheless, middle-age zest is proportionate to middle-age risk.

I have heard people who were reflecting on those years say, "That was when we were really living, when we were most alive."

The Ambassador for Christ finds himself in exactly this middle situation. He stands between the Good News of the Re-creative Christ and the world where his life is spent. He is confronted with other versions of good news which he must hear and evaluate, and he is confronted with bad news and illusory schemes. He must try fairly to understand and interpret both the Word and the world. He stands between competing closed systems which beguile people with their promises of security. He seeks to be a dialogical person among groups more skilled at shouting than conversing. He also stands between the traditional forms of his organism and the necessary reforming which must be done if the organism is to maintain health and performance. He is a bridge builder, and he discovers the risks of the job.

Ambassadors, like adults, feel that they have much to say. But they find themselves in a position where their capacity to listen is perhaps more important than their capacity to speak. The most helpful adults are those who show they are *with* and *for* adolescents, as the adolescents make their own discoveries and learn through their own mistakes. The ambassador's most difficult and most necessary prayer will be the words of St. Francis: "O Lord, make us instruments of your peace . . . help us not so much to seek to be understood, as to understand."

The Ambassador's Perils

Maintaining the tension is no easy matter. The ambassador faces two special perils. He may relax the tension at either end, thus making life easier. But when he succumbs, he forfeits his usefulness as an ambassador. The two perils are: to spend a disproportionate amount of time enjoying the conviviality of the cocktail circuit with his own kind of people; or to give up his commission and simply "go native."

Ambassadors for Christ have always faced the temptation

to spend their major energies in the security of their own ghetto-like compound. In the face of the chaotic, unresponsive world, there is something reassuring about being with the like-minded, especially in an alien culture. Churches tend toward introversion. Those who would be Ambassadors for Christ may find it is quite possible to be diverted from their main tasks by the very bread and wine of the numerous "embassy" celebrations! But the first order of the day must be the task of communication. If we are to be Ambassadors for Christ, we need to be finding out what must be shared and how to share it.

During the early days of the Kennedy administration some new-style ambassadors began to influence American embassies overseas. One of these was John Scott Everton in Burma. One of his earliest changes was to arrange classes in Burmese for American personnel—*the first thing in the morning.* This priority was concrete evidence that the embassy existed for communication; the other's language was our concern.

Ambassadors for Christ cannot do their job if their time is consumed within the "embassy" circle. An early morning priority must go to learning the language of the world to which they are sent.

"Going native" has seldom been an equal threat to ambassadors. Their connections with the commissioning country have usually been too strong. But perhaps for Ambassadors for Christ today, this temptation is more subtle than that of the ghetto or the cocktail circuit. A strong passion to escape the religious ghetto has coincided with the appeal of numerous types of "secular theology." On the whole this reaction has been a healthy one. But given this reaction, today's ambassadors may have to work harder at hearing again "what to share" as well as sharpening their tools of communication. Ambassadors can never take for granted that they "have" the Good News or are in control of the Creative Spirit. Being open to the Word is as necessary and difficult as being open to the world.

Ambassadors must resist the temptations to be confined to

the compound, or to give up the mission. They do this by taking both ends seriously and maintaining the divinely intended tension. Ambassadors are Our Lord the Spirit's People in Brooklyn, Berkeley, Burma, and Beirut.

The Ambassador's Privileges

Tension and peril are the cost side of the rich, many-faceted life of the Ambassador for Christ. But he need not be pitied because of the risks; he can be envied because of the fullness and variety of his opportunities.

Ambassadors live on the frontiers where history is being made. Their work helps to shape the course of history.

Ambassadors for Christ, by their day's work, help to shape history; from the inside this is seen as His-story—the story of Christ's impact shaping the direction of life.

The ambassador is primarily a man of affairs or action. He is not a recluse who contemplates the historical scene from the distance and safety of a balcony. He is in the action on the road. He knows with Dag Hammarskjöld that "In our era, the road to holiness necessarily passes through the world of action." [1]

The ambassador does not make all the key decisions of course. He is not the Lord of history. But his work is part of the network of impressions and decisions. He is no manipulator. He is a workman in the area of human relations, the area where history is made. He works with a quiet confidence that his labors are not in vain.

The master-image of an ambassador does not, of course, provide detailed prescriptions for the performance of the task as it must be worked out in the personal histories of housewives, lawyers, farmers, and professors. Each in his own post will find his usefulness through a Spirit-quickened imagination and costly fidelity to the duty at hand. This will be the way the Ambassador for Christ takes part in history's (His-story's) unfolding.

[1] Dag Hammarskjöld, *Markings* (New York: Alfred A. Knopf, Inc., 1964), p. 122.

Ambassadors live surrounded by the stimulus to lifelong learning. The days are never long enough to search into all the interests that are aroused.

Ambassadors for Christ live on frontier outposts which provide endless stimulus for learning. One of their earliest designations was "disciples" or learners.

Take, for instance, the ambassador living in Rangoon, Burma, on the frontier where the Way of the Christ and the Way of the Buddha meet. There is constant stimulation for learning in *two* directions at *once*. The Ambassador for Christ will want to learn the background of the customs of the people. He will want to know of the life of the Buddha, the favorite books of Buddhist people, the meaning of festivals, the use of pagodas, and how Buddhism and politics are intermingled in Asia today.

But this stimulation will force him back to a deeper study of the home country, which has commissioned him. He will look again at the story of the Christ in the light of the story of the Buddha. He will be concerned with the history of Christ's mission in other countries and cultures. He will be concerned with the fresh thinking and experiments which are going on in other outposts.

The Ambassador for Christ will find stimulus to know his own tradition better, even as he attempts to understand the tradition and the culture of the country where his embassy is located. This two-sided learning will take place regardless of the location of his outpost.

Above the desk of the Ambassador for Christ will be found the motto: *Homo Sum: Humani Nihil A Me Alienum Puto,* "I am a man; nothing human is alien to me."

But the stimulus to a life of learning will have a practical application. This learning is not simply for the sake of more research. It is learning with a view to being a more understanding and effective ambassador. If the ambassador is a constantly growing person, it is because his life provides the occasion and motivation for lifelong learning in many directions.

Ambassadors' days are filled with varied contacts with all kinds of people. Since they are ambassadors wherever they go, no encounter is without potential significance.

Ambassadors for Christ live as "people-persons." Their days are made up of encounters and relationships with people. Wherever they are, they find the days filled with a never-ending series of human interactions which give opportunities for embassy service and occasions for personal expansion.

The Ambassador for Christ is never off duty. Even his holidays find him representing the third-race, which has commissioned him. Consequently, his life always knows tension. But the tensions are divinely intended and need not paralyze him. They are actually the source of the richness of his days.

Increasingly the Ambassador for Christ finds his life and work to be of one piece. His joy comes from his work; he likes his job. He does not need a holiday in order to strip off an oppressive "role." The Ambassador for Christ is not role-playing. Being "all of one piece," he is real in all of his relationships.

Ambassadors fill one post at a time. They are not responsible for the whole world! They must be prepared to stay or move, depending upon the directives given them.

Ambassadors for Christ give themselves to concrete tasks. Their outpost is only one of many. Their contribution to the whole world (ecumenical service) is made through their faithfulness to their commissioned task. They must be prepared to "dig in" or to move quickly, depending upon the Spirit's directives.

In this way, the ambassador can believe in the significance of his work, knowing that his mission is a part of a much larger mission. He will neither exaggerate nor denigrate the importance of his particular task. He is required only to be faithful. No matter what the pressures may be, he can live with a certain "light touch"; he knows what Reinhold Niebuhr liked to call the "nonchalance of faith."

At times he may wish he had more control over his future.

But he is not his own man. He is bound in service to Our Lord the Spirit. Responsiveness and flexibility to the Spirit's direction mark him; even as a Spirit-inspired curiosity to learn and understand mark him. But increasingly he comes to learn that being bound to the Spirit's service is really the greatest freedom. His most zestful and rewarding experience comes *through* this service, not outside of it. He is most truly himself when he is most responsive to the Spirit.

Ambassadors know the camaraderie of a team. They work with others. When they are gone, others will carry on where they have left off. No matter how difficult the assignment, the sense of working together with great colleagues is one of their richest rewards.

Ambassadors for Christ know the rich *esprit de corps* of their fellow ambassadors. They are not lonely, isolated workers. They are fellow workers with each other and with the Creative Spirit, who has called and commissioned them. Their struggles are shared, even as their joys. The banquet table is the symbol of their life together. They enjoy nothing as much as a good celebration.

This camaraderie in work assures criticism and correction if one person's work is out of line. It assures continuity when one ambassador leaves and another follows. The work continues.

Fellow embassy members strengthen each other through mutual criticism and discipline. This may not always be easy to take or understand at the time. But the group's wisdom and concern take priority over individual judgments. In the end, participation in the community is seen to be the source of strength and usefulness.

Perhaps the richest reward is to have been in a significant engagement with supporting and strengthening colleagues. In the thick of the struggle when great issues were at stake, they experience a unique bond: "We were in it together." Looking back while at some future banquet, we will say, "Those were great days; we were really living!"

Leon Bloy, the French Catholic convert, once wrote: "There

is only one misery; not to be saints." To live but not to be "transparent to the Divine" is really to have missed it, for being saints—participants in His-story—is what life is all about.

In a similar way it can be said, *there is only one misery— not to be Ambassadors for Christ.* To live, but not to be rooted in the Creative Center, living openly between the old, closed worlds, as an emissary of the fresh, new era— this is misery.

The Ambassador Between the Yogi and the Commissar

We have been looking at three dominant images in our day: the Yogi, the Commissar, and the Ambassador. But how are they related to each other?

My intention has been to provide a discussion starter, not an answer-book. As a teacher my concern is with the quality of the discussion, not the acceptance of some neat formula. At the same time, it would have been impossible (and inauthentic!) to disguise my enthusiasm for the prospect of the Ambassador's existence.

I believe the Ambassador finds his greatest test today in standing between the Yogi and the Commissar. This position will test his capacity to listen with respect and understanding. The Yogi, with his timeless wisdom and newly appreciated message, must be taken seriously. The Commissar has revolutionized much of the modern world; his influence is growing, not diminishing. To be rooted in the Center will not mean to dismiss these with hasty insensitivity. On the contrary, loyalty to the Christ, or the Truth, should result in a sympathetic and critical hearing and a concern to understand. Concern for Truth should lead to freedom from defensiveness or coercive aggressiveness.

But the Ambassador for Christ will not be blind or sentimental. His listening will sharpen his sense of discrimination, his capacity for seeing important differences. The way of the Ambassador will be seen to contrast at crucial points with the ways of the Yogi and the Commissar. The careful and fair explanation of these differences will also be a part of his task of understanding and mediation.

But the further he pursues the path of respectful hearing and careful discrimination, the clearer will emerge the sense of the Third-World Church as *ultimately inclusive*. The deeper he draws from the Center where the Christ is the portrait of the Creative Spirit, the deeper he will sense his kinship with all men. He can rejoice in affirming the best elements wherever found and under whatever name. At the same time, he will not shirk the task of warning when he sees disintegrating dangers.

He has begun to experience that "Home" which is "a home for the hearts of all men." In this Home the front door is always open, a fire lights the hearth, and there are ample stores of bread and wine.

Pilgrims and dusty travelers from many roads come from East and West, from Left and Right. From their ways they discover the Way which leads Home. And as they enter, they hear the singing of a new song. They discover in the Home that they are brothers and sisters, and they will rejoice, "We are one in the Spirit, we are one in the Lord." [2]

[2] Peter Scholtes, "They'll Know We Are Christians." © Copyright 1966, F. E. L. Publications, Ltd., Los Angeles, California.

Epilogue
On Getting in the Way

In my teens I heard an evangelist tell the story of his conversion to Christ. The story has continued to amuse and haunt me for the last thirty years.

He related that when he was a boy, there came a day when a large tent was pitched on the edge of his town. Taking the tent to be a circus tent, he went out one night and carefully crawled under the canvas to watch the show. But to his great amazement, when he got inside, he found it was not a circus but an old-fashioned revival meeting. However, once in, he was too embarrassed to leave; so he stayed for the meeting. In the course of the service he came to feel that the message was directed right to him. When the invitation was given at the close of the service, he responded. For him, the Christian life began that night. Eventually he became an evangelist.

In my youth I was very skeptical of the story. It sounded phony! It seemed too slick to be real. I wondered if he had made it up or retouched it to give it a dramatic effect.

Later I became slightly more tolerant and was willing to

concede that maybe it did happen that way to him. But this gave *me* little help. Conversion had certainly not come that way in my case. I wondered if anyone could be so certain of the time, place, and circumstances of the beginning of the Christian life. Having been nurtured in a Christian home, I could not recall a time when I did not believe; but also there was never a time when I was not *also* an unbeliever. Believing and doubting were as intertwined with me as doing good and doing evil. Any interpretation of the Christian life that did not take into account my "mixed" existence was of no help to *me*.

But as I continue to think about the evangelist's story, I have come to be less concerned about the details or his motives. The story appears to me now, more and more, as a parable of Everyman who is a participant in the Third-World Church. Every conscious member of the third-race has been contacted and "drawn in" originally through some very earthy, imperfect means, as mundane or accidental as crawling under the tent.

Some were taken to a local church by their parents, and at the time they thought it was boring beyond words. Some attended a youth group, largely because of the gang, and especially because of the little girl with black hair. Some came in touch with the "living tradition of faith" through a summer camp, because there was an opening at that period and the camp was inexpensive. Some contacted a college-age discussion group where it was possible to discuss social problems in a free atmosphere. Some adults contacted the movement when, in a crisis situation, a long-time trusted friend was the very strength of God.

But, through whatever means, contact was made with a participant in the Way.

Actually, all participants are a *mixture* of the new and the old, the believer and the doubter, the saint and the sinner. We never meet the *unmixed!* The new Way comes to us embodied in people and experiences which are parts of our ongoing history. We make responses in these experiences as we say a yes or no to life. Only later do we come to see that our responses were not simply to Life in the abstract; we were responding to the creative outreach of Our Lord the Spirit.

From such accumulated moments of response, we are shaped. In these moments "we give ourselves away." We are found to be fearful, cowardly, or superficial; or we are becoming open, questing, and adventuresome. In our responses we are saying a yes or a no to Life, to the Giver of Life.

Out of such responses as these, our life in the Third-World Church begins; and through such continued yes-saying, our participation continues.

Our continuance contains the same mystery as our entrance. We are never coerced into continuing. We can turn a deaf ear, drop out, or through lack of discipline become so insensitive as not to know a full-blown crisis when it is upon us. But the mystery of the call and the response remains. The call is also prior to our response. Our Lord the Spirit opens new doors, places new demands upon us, thrusts us into situations calling for fresh decisions and risks. Then we can be remade, reshaped, and re-created through a yes-response to Life. Or we can, through a sluggish no, become hardened, closed, and dull. The mystery forever remains why we choose the lower when the higher is available, why we swap paradise for apple pie. But the wonder also increases that even if we are twisted, shriveled people, we can be re-created through life-giving encounters which somehow come to us.

But in the mystery of the re-creating Life, even our yes-saying seems more a gift than an achievement. We sense that we are enabled, empowered, to open to Life, in spite of every inclination to close or procrastinate.

Our sneaking under the tent seems not *wholly* accidental. It is as if, in spite of our foolish antics, we were being drawn to hear and then enabled to respond. It is as if we were "grasped" and so were made into Good-News people, who embody, however imperfectly, the dawn of the new age.

In the face of the Yogi and the Commissar we are respectful, but we are not ashamed. Rather, we are grateful and joyful for the prospect of a New Way.

Dag Hammarskjöld wrote in his *Markings* in 1956:

—Lead us not into temptation,
But deliver us from evil:
Let all that is in me serve Thee,
And *thus* free me from all fear.

You dare your Yes—and experience a meaning.
You repeat your Yes—and all things acquire a meaning.
When everything has a meaning,
how can you live anything but a *Yes*.[1]

[1] Dag Hammarskjöld, *Markings* (New York: Alfred A. Knopf, Inc., 1964), p. 125.